THE

High 5

DAILY JOURNAL

FIRST EDITION

Published in the United States by: Hay House, Inc.: www.hayhouse.com® • Published in
Australia by: Hay House Australia Pty. Ltd.: www.hayhouse.com.au • Published in the United
Kingdom by: Hay House UK, Ltd.: www.hayhouse.co.uk • Published in India by: Hay House
Publishers India: www.hayhouse.co.in

Content Production: Tracey Merz and Nancy Hala
Cover & Interior design: Skye High Interactive, Inc.
Interior photos: Jenny Moloney

Hardcover ISBN (US): 978-1-4019-6342-2

Hardcover ISBN (UK): 978-1-7881-7617-0

10 9 8 7 6 5 4 3 2 1
1st edition, November 2021
Printed in Korea

THE

High 5

DAILY JOURNAL

MEL ROBBINS

HAY HOUSE, INC.
Carlsbad, California • New York City
London • Sydney • New Delhi

It's time to start believing in yourself again.

Name: _____

Date: _____/_____/_____

Describe what's happening in your life right now and what you want to change over the next three months:

In this daily journal, you'll find the secret to forging a deeper connection with yourself.

This simple journaling method is grounded in science and will help you lower stress, gain clarity, and motivate you to take daily action. Because taking small steps every day in the direction of your goals and dreams is the magic formula to fulfillment.

Using this journal, you will build the discipline, confidence, and habits you need to know that you can always count on yourself. Face any challenge. Surmount any obstacle. You'll see yourself waking up every day, inching closer to what you want, and becoming the person you know you were born to be.

Even more than productivity, you'll experience greater transformation the more you use the prompts in this journal.

They are designed to calm your nervous system, open your mind, and ignite your intuition so it can lead you where you're meant to go.

And with your beautifully designed body-mind-spirit working in harmony, there's nothing in the world you can't do, make, be or have. Fulfillment in all areas of life is your birthright. It's what you're here for.

As you embark on this journey, I want you to know that you are about to create the one thing we all want. The thing we all wish for those we love dearly and deeply. That thing we need to envision and create for ourselves:

A life worth celebrating.

Mel

Confidence

Confidence is not some magical alchemy of traits reserved for the most successful, influential, and famous among us. Confidence is within all of us. It's within YOU. You were born with it.

If you've lost confidence in yourself—in any area of your life or on any level—all that means is you are temporarily blocked from the feeling of it. You can't put your finger on it, but something, maybe everything, just seems off, out of balance, out of sync.

Over time, because you're blocked from the feeling of confidence, your mind begins to block your belief in it. That's what makes you scared and insecure, filled with self-doubt and worry. Your mind is now following your body, and they're both working against you.

Guess what happens next? Your spirit stops in its tracks. Your internal guidance system has one purpose only, and that is to lead you in the direction of your dreams. But now you feel cut off from your dreams and begin to tell yourself they will never happen for you.

Why? Because your body and your mind are doing the opposite of what they're designed to do: they are blocking your spirit instead of holding the door open for it. Your spirit wants to soar. Those miserable feelings are your intelligent design system banging on the door, telling you to open it back up.

That's where *The High 5 Daily Journal* comes in.

Build a Confident Body, Mind, and Spirit

Confidence runs deeper than you think. It runs through your body, mind, and spirit. This journal uses science to teach you how to create all three kinds of confidence.

A confident body means being comfortable in your own skin—knowing how to calm yourself and soothe your nerves:

- Feeling grounded and present
- Stable and strong
- Rooted in self-awareness
- Ready for action

A confident mind sees the world in full, vivid color and trusts in your ability to face whatever may come your way:

- Believing in yourself
- Spotting opportunities for what's meant for you
- Feeling inspired and optimistic
- Trusting in the divine nature of things

A confident spirit wants to try new things and soar, unfettered, toward its destiny:

- Courageous and expressive
- Eager to be seen, heard and acknowledged
- Always learning and leaning toward it's desires
- Filled with joy and celebration

When your body, mind, and spirit are lined up, your senses come alive, your mind focuses, and your heart expands. You are fully present.

That is High 5 Energy.

Unlock The Most Powerful Force in the World — YOU.

Backed By Powerful Science

The exercises in this journal are based on research and evidence. These daily practices in confidence, visualization, and mindset will change your brain's neural pathways and create new habits that will transform every aspect of your life.

Empower Your Confident Body, Mind, and Spirit

Following the steps outlined in this journal, you will tap into your natural confidence and let it flow through your body, enhance your mind, and awaken your spirit. The more you use this journal, the faster confidence becomes a habit.

Simple Discipline, Profound Results

These exercises are simple, but over time their impact on your life will be profound. New ways of acting lead to different ways of thinking and feeling. In the beginning, these changes are *things you do*, and over time, they become a part of *who you are*.

Believe In Your Dreams Again

Your dreams are out there waiting for you. But you need to believe in them and take action. This daily journal will train your body, mind, and spirit to both pick up on the clues life is sending you and cultivate the courage to move toward them.

Celebrate Your Life

It's pretty simple: you're not cheering yourself forward and that's holding you back. With this journal, every day you'll be more present to who you are, what you want, and how you show up. By cheering for yourself, and developing the habits to keep cheering no matter what, you will burst through what's blocking you.

1

Thanks to neuroscience, we know a stressed-out body puts your brain in survival mode and shows you threats instead of opportunities. So, all change requires you to settle your body first.

2

Take a deep breath. It's a powerful way to settle your nervous system, because it activates your vagus nerve. It's your secret weapon to creating instant calm in your body.

3

Hands on your heart is another way to tone your vagus nerve. This mantra is how you teach your body what it feels like to be safe and settled and access your calm and cool center.

4

Your senses are a conduit for the energy of your spirit. Begin to awaken that energy now to listen to it later.

5

Naming how your body feels is a key step toward deeper self-awareness and feeling comfortable with yourself.

6

My favorite daily habit to rewire the filter in your mind is to tell yourself that *you're worth cheering for, your dreams matter, and you can handle whatever comes your way.*

7

Once your body is calm, you can focus your mind and attention where you want it to go.

TODAY'S DATE: 12 / 5

Settle Your Body

Ground yourself in the present moment to get comfortable in your own skin.

✓ Take a deep breath

✓ Put your hands on your heart and say "I'm okay, I'm safe, I'm loved"

✓ What's one thing you can

See _I see bare trees out the window_   Hear _I hear my dog barking_

Touch _I feel my pen in my hand_   Smell _I smell freshly brewed coffee_

✓ In one word, I feel... _Busy_

✓ I deserve a High 5 today because _I got up on time this morning!_

✓ The next time you pass a mirror, prove it. Give yourself a High 5! 🖐

Clear Your Mind

To cultivate a confident mind, clear it of everything that's filling it right now: worries, tasks, doodles, thoughts, ideas, to-dos, or anything you don't want to forget.

Today is packed at work and I'm up against a big deadline. The dog needs to go out and is looking at me with these big eyes but I'll take her out as soon as I finish this. I need to call my mom back, she called and I feel guilty for not having called but I need to finish this deadline first. I woke up and immediately felt stressed by everything on my plate but I'm so glad I didn't look at my phone this morning and exercised to put myself first.

8

Clear your mind. Dump all your thoughts out onto the page. Don't hold back. Get it out of your head so that you can get into the present moment with yourself.

9

Now your body is calm and your mind is clear. It's time to awaken your spirit.

10

Start dreaming in the morning! Write down five things that you want. Believe in them. Give yourself permission to have exactly what you desire.

Free Your Spirit

A confident spirit is celebrating yourself and moving toward your desires.
Give yourself permission to get in touch with what you WANT.

WRITE 5 THINGS YOU WANT:

Big or small. Today or in your lifetime.

To free up my day to have more time for myself

To go on a trip every year to somewhere new

To get in the best shape of my life

To start a nonprofit related to improving mental health

To learn how to meditate and become more mindful

11

Writing what you want will start to shift what you believe is possible as you rewire the filter in your mind. It also leads to a 42% higher chance of achieving your dreams!

escribe the small actions you could take to inch closer to the things you want.

More time for myself - I can schedule it into my calendar. I can set a time when I'll stop working and stick to it. I can make a plan to do a yoga class with a friend. I'll keep filling out my daily journal every morning. I am going to wake up earlier and use that time to work on writing a plan for the nonprofit.

12

Most people get manifesting wrong because they try to visualize the end result. Neuroscience research tells us to visualize yourself doing the hard, annoying, small steps along the way to reaching your dreams. In doing so, you tell your brain, "I do the hard work. I take advantage of opportunities. And I don't back down, I take action.

NOW CLOSE YOUR EYES

Visualize taking these small actions.
eel deeply what it feels like to do these things and move closer to what you desire.
This trains your body, mind, and spirit to help you take these actions.

13

Brain scans have shown that you stimulate the same regions in your brain when you visualize yourself performing an action as when you actually do that same action, which makes you more likely to follow through on that action. And it's your actions that get results.

THE

High 5

DAILY JOURNAL

CELEBRATE YOURSELF

You deserve to be celebrated for who you are, where you are, right now, starting today. By intentionally and deliberately cheering for yourself, and developing the habits to keep cheering no matter what, you can burst through everything that's holding you back.

Settle Your Body

Ground yourself in the present moment to get comfortable in your own skin.

Take a deep breath

Put your hands on your heart and say "I'm okay, I'm safe, I'm loved"

What's one thing you can

See _paintings_   Hear _buzzing_

Touch _Book_   Smell _pineapple_

In one word, I feel... _hungry_

I deserve a High 5 today because _____

The next time you pass a mirror, prove it. Give yourself a High 5!

Clear Your Mind

To cultivate a confident mind, clear it of everything that's filling it right now: worries, tasks, doodles, thoughts, ideas, to-dos, or anything you don't want to forget.

Free Your Spirit

A confident spirit is celebrating yourself and moving toward your desires.

Give yourself permission to get in touch with what you WANT.

WRITE 5 THINGS YOU WANT:

Big or small. Today or in your lifetime.

1. Sell paintings
2. Learn how to budget
3. Stay positive
4. don't get depressed.
5. don't worry. Be happy.

Describe the small actions you could take to inch closer to the things you want.

NOW CLOSE YOUR EYES

Visualize taking these small actions.

Feel deeply what it feels like to do these things and move closer to what you desire.

This trains your body, mind, and spirit to help you take these actions.

Settle Your Body

Ground yourself in the present moment to get comfortable in your own skin.

- [ ] Take a deep breath
- [ ] Put your hands on your heart and say "I'm okay, I'm safe, I'm loved"
- [ ] What's one thing you can

See _____   Hear _____

Touch _____   Smell _____

- [ ] In one word, I feel... _____
- [ ] I deserve a High 5 today because _____
- [ ] The next time you pass a mirror, prove it. Give yourself a High 5! 👏

Clear Your Mind

To cultivate a confident mind, clear it of everything that's filling it right now: worries, tasks, doodles, thoughts, ideas, to-dos, or anything you don't want to forget.

Free Your Spirit

A confident spirit is celebrating yourself and moving toward your desires.

Give yourself permission to get in touch with what you WANT.

WRITE 5 THINGS YOU WANT:

Big or small. Today or in your lifetime.

1. _____

2. _____

3. _____

4. _____

5. _____

Describe the small actions you could take to inch closer to the things you want.

-

-

-

-

-

-

-

-

NOW CLOSE YOUR EYES

Visualize taking these small actions.

Feel deeply what it feels like to do these things and move closer to what you desire.
This trains your body, mind, and spirit to help you take these actions.

Settle Your Body

Ground yourself in the present moment to get comfortable in your own skin.

☐ Take a deep breath

☐ Put your hands on your heart and say "I'm okay, I'm safe, I'm loved"

☐ What's one thing you can

See _____   Hear _____

Touch _____   Smell _____

☐ In one word, I feel... _____

☐ I deserve a High 5 today because _____

☐ The next time you pass a mirror, prove it. Give yourself a High 5! 👋

Clear Your Mind

To cultivate a confident mind, clear it of everything that's filling it right now: worries, tasks, doodles, thoughts, ideas, to-dos, or anything you don't want to forget.

Free Your Spirit

Big or small. Today or in your lifetime.

1. _____

2. _____

3. _____

4. _____

5. _____

Describe the small actions you could take to inch closer to the things you want.

NOW CLOSE YOUR EYES

Visualize taking these small actions.
Feel deeply what it feels like to do these things and move closer to what you desire.
This trains your body, mind, and spirit to help you take these actions.

Settle Your Body

Ground yourself in the present moment to get comfortable in your own skin.

- Take a deep breath
- Put your hands on your heart and say "I'm okay, I'm safe, I'm loved"
- What's one thing you can

See _____   Hear _____

Touch _____   Smell _____

- In one word, I feel... _____
- I deserve a High 5 today because _____
- The next time you pass a mirror, prove it. Give yourself a High 5! 🖐️

Clear Your Mind

To cultivate a confident mind, clear it of everything that's filling it right now: worries, tasks, doodles, thoughts, ideas, to-dos, or anything you don't want to forget.

Free Your Spirit

Big or small. Today or in your lifetime.

1. _____

2. _____

3. _____

4. _____

5. _____

Describe the small actions you could take to inch closer to the things you want.

Visualize taking these small actions.
Feel deeply what it feels like to do these things and move closer to what you desire.
This trains your body, mind, and spirit to help you take these actions.

Settle Your Body

Ground yourself in the present moment to get comfortable in your own skin.

- Take a deep breath
- Put your hands on your heart and say "I'm okay, I'm safe, I'm loved"
- What's one thing you can

See _____   Hear _____

Touch _____   Smell _____

- In one word, I feel... _____
- I deserve a High 5 today because _____
- The next time you pass a mirror, prove it. Give yourself a High 5! 🖐️

Clear Your Mind

To cultivate a confident mind, clear it of everything that's filling it right now: worries, tasks, doodles, thoughts, ideas, to-dos, or anything you don't want to forget.

Free Your Spirit

Big or small. Today or in your lifetime.

1. _____

2. _____

3. _____

4. _____

5. _____

Describe the small actions you could take to inch closer to the things you want.

NOW CLOSE YOUR EYES

Visualize taking these small actions.
Feel deeply what it feels like to do these things and move closer to what you desire.
This trains your body, mind, and spirit to help you take these actions.

Settle Your Body

Ground yourself in the present moment to get comfortable in your own skin.

- Take a deep breath
- Put your hands on your heart and say "I'm okay, I'm safe, I'm loved"
- What's one thing you can

See _____ Hear _____

Touch _____ Smell _____

- In one word, I feel... _____

- I deserve a High 5 today because _____

- The next time you pass a mirror, prove it. Give yourself a High 5! 👐

Clear Your Mind

To cultivate a confident mind, clear it of everything that's filling it right now: worries, tasks, doodles, thoughts, ideas, to-dos, or anything you don't want to forget.

Free Your Spirit

Big or small. Today or in your lifetime.

1. _____

2. _____

3. _____

4. _____

5. _____

Describe the small actions you could take to inch closer to the things you want.

-
-
-
-
-
-
-

NOW CLOSE YOUR EYES

Visualize taking these small actions.
Feel deeply what it feels like to do these things and move closer to what you desire.
This trains your body, mind, and spirit to help you take these actions.

Settle Your Body

Ground yourself in the present moment to get comfortable in your own skin.

☐ Take a deep breath

☐ Put your hands on your heart and say "I'm okay, I'm safe, I'm loved"

☐ What's one thing you can

See _____   Hear _____

Touch _____   Smell _____

☐ In one word, I feel... _____

☐ I deserve a High 5 today because _____

☐ The next time you pass a mirror, prove it. Give yourself a High 5!

Clear Your Mind

To cultivate a confident mind, clear it of everything that's filling it right now: worries, tasks, doodles, thoughts, ideas, to-dos, or anything you don't want to forget.

-
-
-
-
-
-
-
-
-

Free Your Spirit

Big or small. Today or in your lifetime.

1. _____

2. _____

3. _____

4. _____

5. _____

Describe the small actions you could take to inch closer to the things you want.

-
-
-
-
-
-
-

NOW CLOSE YOUR EYES

Visualize taking these small actions.
Feel deeply what it feels like to do these things and move closer to what you desire.
This trains your body, mind, and spirit to help you take these actions.

I'm so proud of you for finishing your first week of *The High 5 Daily Journal.*

Your turn! Now take a photo of yourself giving me a High 5. Tag me and post it.

@melrobbins

YOUR DREAMS MATTER

Dreams are encoded in your DNA, they are spoken by the soul, but they are remembered by the mind. Dreams don't disappear. That means you take them with you, wherever you go, and in whatever version of yourself you create. So you might as well stop running and start leaning into them. You might as well see and hear and feel all the clues your life is giving you about who you are destined to be. Your dreams are much bigger and more amazing than you can even imagine.

Settle Your Body

Ground yourself in the present moment to get comfortable in your own skin.

- [ ] Take a deep breath
- [ ] Put your hands on your heart and say "I'm okay, I'm safe, I'm loved"
- [ ] What's one thing you can

See _____   Hear _____

Touch _____   Smell _____

- [ ] In one word, I feel... _____
- [ ] I deserve a High 5 today because _____
- [ ] The next time you pass a mirror, prove it. Give yourself a High 5! 🖐

Clear Your Mind

To cultivate a confident mind, clear it of everything that's filling it right now: worries, tasks, doodles, thoughts, ideas, to-dos, or anything you don't want to forget.

Free Your Spirit

WRITE 5 THINGS YOU WANT:

Big or small. Today or in your lifetime.

1. _____

2. _____

3. _____

4. _____

5. _____

Describe the small actions you could take to inch closer to the things you want.

-
-
-
-
-
-
-

NOW CLOSE YOUR EYES

Visualize taking these small actions.

Feel deeply what it feels like to do these things and move closer to what you desire.

This trains your body, mind, and spirit to help you take these actions.

Settle Your Body

Ground yourself in the present moment to get comfortable in your own skin.

- [ ] Take a deep breath
- [ ] Put your hands on your heart and say "I'm okay, I'm safe, I'm loved"
- [ ] What's one thing you can

See _____   Hear _____

Touch _____   Smell _____

- [ ] In one word, I feel... _____
- [ ] I deserve a High 5 today because _____
- [ ] The next time you pass a mirror, prove it. Give yourself a High 5! 🙌

Clear Your Mind

To cultivate a confident mind, clear it of everything that's filling it right now: worries, tasks, doodles, thoughts, ideas, to-dos, or anything you don't want to forget.

- ▪
- ▪
- ▪
- ▪
- ▪
- ▪
- ▪
- ▪
- ▪

Free Your Spirit

Big or small. Today or in your lifetime.

1. _____

2. _____

3. _____

4. _____

5. _____

Describe the small actions you could take to inch closer to the things you want.

NOW CLOSE YOUR EYES

Visualize taking these small actions.

Feel deeply what it feels like to do these things and move closer to what you desire.

This trains your body, mind, and spirit to help you take these actions.

Settle Your Body

Ground yourself in the present moment to get comfortable in your own skin.

- [ ] Take a deep breath
- [ ] Put your hands on your heart and say "I'm okay, I'm safe, I'm loved"
- [ ] What's one thing you can

  See _____   Hear _____

  Touch _____   Smell _____

- [ ] In one word, I feel... _____
- [ ] I deserve a High 5 today because _____
- [ ] The next time you pass a mirror, prove it. Give yourself a High 5! 👏

Clear Your Mind

To cultivate a confident mind, clear it of everything that's filling it right now: worries, tasks, doodles, thoughts, ideas, to-dos, or anything you don't want to forget.

Free Your Spirit

Big or small. Today or in your lifetime.

1. _____

2. _____

3. _____

4. _____

5. _____

Describe the small actions you could take to inch closer to the things you want.

NOW CLOSE YOUR EYES

Visualize taking these small actions.
Feel deeply what it feels like to do these things and move closer to what you desire.
This trains your body, mind, and spirit to help you take these actions.

Settle Your Body

Ground yourself in the present moment to get comfortable in your own skin.

☐ Take a deep breath

☐ Put your hands on your heart and say "I'm okay, I'm safe, I'm loved"

☐ What's one thing you can

See _____   Hear _____

Touch _____   Smell _____

☐ In one word, I feel... _____

☐ I deserve a High 5 today because _____

☐ The next time you pass a mirror, prove it. Give yourself a High 5! 🙌

Clear Your Mind

To cultivate a confident mind, clear it of everything that's filling it right now: worries, tasks, doodles, thoughts, ideas, to-dos, or anything you don't want to forget.

Free Your Spirit

Big or small. Today or in your lifetime.

1. _____

2. _____

3. _____

4. _____

5. _____

Describe the small actions you could take to inch closer to the things you want.

NOW CLOSE YOUR EYES

Visualize taking these small actions.

Feel deeply what it feels like to do these things and move closer to what you desire.

This trains your body, mind, and spirit to help you take these actions.

Settle Your Body

Ground yourself in the present moment to get comfortable in your own skin.

☐ Take a deep breath

☐ Put your hands on your heart and say "I'm okay, I'm safe, I'm loved"

☐ What's one thing you can

See _____ Hear _____

Touch _____ Smell _____

☐ In one word, I feel... _____

☐ I deserve a High 5 today because _____

☐ The next time you pass a mirror, prove it. Give yourself a High 5! 👏

Clear Your Mind

To cultivate a confident mind, clear it of everything that's filling it right now: worries, tasks, doodles, thoughts, ideas, to-dos, or anything you don't want to forget.

Free Your Spirit

Big or small. Today or in your lifetime.

1. _____

2. _____

3. _____

4. _____

5. _____

Describe the small actions you could take to inch closer to the things you want.

NOW CLOSE YOUR EYES

Visualize taking these small actions.
Feel deeply what it feels like to do these things and move closer to what you desire.
This trains your body, mind, and spirit to help you take these actions.

Settle Your Body

Ground yourself in the present moment to get comfortable in your own skin.

☐ Take a deep breath

☐ Put your hands on your heart and say "I'm okay, I'm safe, I'm loved"

☐ What's one thing you can

See _____ Hear _____

Touch _____ Smell _____

☐ In one word, I feel... _____

☐ I deserve a High 5 today because _____

☐ The next time you pass a mirror, prove it. Give yourself a High 5! 🙌

Clear Your Mind

To cultivate a confident mind, clear it of everything that's filling it right now: worries, tasks, doodles, thoughts, ideas, to-dos, or anything you don't want to forget.

Free Your Spirit

Big or small. Today or in your lifetime.

1. _____

2. _____

3. _____

4. _____

5. _____

Describe the small actions you could take to inch closer to the things you want.

Visualize taking these small actions.
Feel deeply what it feels like to do these things and move closer to what you desire.
This trains your body, mind, and spirit to help you take these actions.

Settle Your Body

Ground yourself in the present moment to get comfortable in your own skin.

- [ ] Take a deep breath
- [ ] Put your hands on your heart and say "I'm okay, I'm safe, I'm loved"
- [ ] What's one thing you can

See _____   Hear _____

Touch _____   Smell _____

- [ ] In one word, I feel... _____
- [ ] I deserve a High 5 today because _____
- [ ] The next time you pass a mirror, prove it. Give yourself a High 5! 🙌

Clear Your Mind

To cultivate a confident mind, clear it of everything that's filling it right now: worries, tasks, doodles, thoughts, ideas, to-dos, or anything you don't want to forget.

- ▪
- ▪
- ▪
- ▪
- ▪
- ▪
- ▪
- ▪
- ▪

Free Your Spirit

Big or small. Today or in your lifetime.

1. _____

2. _____

3. _____

4. _____

5. _____

Describe the small actions you could take to inch closer to the things you want.

NOW CLOSE YOUR EYES

Visualize taking these small actions.
Feel deeply what it feels like to do these things and move closer to what you desire.
This trains your body, mind, and spirit to help you take these actions.

Doesn't it feel great to cheer for yourself?
I want to celebrate WITH you.

Take everything you're practicing a step further by joining my free 5 day High 5 Challenge at:

High5Challenge.com

YOU ARE
BRAVE

You can feel sure about your dreams and be terrified of them at the same time. There is an art to learning to ride the waves of emotion, the ups and downs, without getting stuck in the low, scary moments. Building your inner confidence gives you the courage to go after what you want, and if you get knocked down, it gives you the resilience to get right back up and keep trying.

Settle Your Body

Ground yourself in the present moment to get comfortable in your own skin.

Take a deep breath

Put your hands on your heart and say "I'm okay, I'm safe, I'm loved"

What's one thing you can

See _____   Hear _____

Touch _____   Smell _____

In one word, I feel... _____

I deserve a High 5 today because _____

The next time you pass a mirror, prove it. Give yourself a High 5! 👋

Clear Your Mind

To cultivate a confident mind, clear it of everything that's filling it right now: worries, tasks, doodles, thoughts, ideas, to-dos, or anything you don't want to forget.

Free Your Spirit

Big or small. Today or in your lifetime.

1. _____

2. _____

3. _____

4. _____

5. _____

Describe the small actions you could take to inch closer to the things you want.

NOW CLOSE YOUR EYES

Visualize taking these small actions.

Feel deeply what it feels like to do these things and move closer to what you desire.

This trains your body, mind, and spirit to help you take these actions.

Settle Your Body

Ground yourself in the present moment to get comfortable in your own skin.

☐ Take a deep breath

☐ Put your hands on your heart and say "I'm okay, I'm safe, I'm loved"

☐ What's one thing you can

See _____   Hear _____

Touch _____   Smell _____

☐ In one word, I feel... _____

☐ I deserve a High 5 today because _____

☐ The next time you pass a mirror, prove it. Give yourself a High 5! 🖐

Clear Your Mind

To cultivate a confident mind, clear it of everything that's filling it right now: worries, tasks, doodles, thoughts, ideas, to-dos, or anything you don't want to forget.

Free Your Spirit

Big or small. Today or in your lifetime.

1. _____

2. _____

3. _____

4. _____

5. _____

Describe the small actions you could take to inch closer to the things you want.

NOW CLOSE YOUR EYES

Visualize taking these small actions.
Feel deeply what it feels like to do these things and move closer to what you desire.
This trains your body, mind, and spirit to help you take these actions.

Settle Your Body

Ground yourself in the present moment to get comfortable in your own skin.

☐ Take a deep breath

☐ Put your hands on your heart and say "I'm okay, I'm safe, I'm loved"

☐ What's one thing you can

See _____   Hear _____

Touch _____   Smell _____

☐ In one word, I feel... _____

☐ I deserve a High 5 today because _____

☐ The next time you pass a mirror, prove it. Give yourself a High 5! 🖐

Clear Your Mind

To cultivate a confident mind, clear it of everything that's filling it right now: worries, tasks, doodles, thoughts, ideas, to-dos, or anything you don't want to forget.

-
-
-
-
-
-
-
-
-

Free Your Spirit

Big or small. Today or in your lifetime.

1. _____

2. _____

3. _____

4. _____

5. _____

Describe the small actions you could take to inch closer to the things you want.

NOW CLOSE YOUR EYES

Visualize taking these small actions.
Feel deeply what it feels like to do these things and move closer to what you desire.
This trains your body, mind, and spirit to help you take these actions.

Settle Your Body

Ground yourself in the present moment to get comfortable in your own skin.

☐ Take a deep breath

☐ Put your hands on your heart and say "I'm okay, I'm safe, I'm loved"

☐ What's one thing you can

See _____   Hear _____

Touch _____   Smell _____

☐ In one word, I feel... _____

☐ I deserve a High 5 today because _____

☐ The next time you pass a mirror, prove it. Give yourself a High 5! 👐

Clear Your Mind

To cultivate a confident mind, clear it of everything that's filling it right now: worries, tasks, doodles, thoughts, ideas, to-dos, or anything you don't want to forget.

Free Your Spirit

Big or small. Today or in your lifetime.

1. _____

2. _____

3. _____

4. _____

5. _____

Describe the small actions you could take to inch closer to the things you want.

NOW CLOSE YOUR EYES

Visualize taking these small actions.
Feel deeply what it feels like to do these things and move closer to what you desire.
This trains your body, mind, and spirit to help you take these actions.

Settle Your Body

Ground yourself in the present moment to get comfortable in your own skin.

- Take a deep breath
- Put your hands on your heart and say "I'm okay, I'm safe, I'm loved"
- What's one thing you can

See _____   Hear _____

Touch _____   Smell _____

- In one word, I feel... _____

- I deserve a High 5 today because _____

- The next time you pass a mirror, prove it. Give yourself a High 5!

Clear Your Mind

To cultivate a confident mind, clear it of everything that's filling it right now: worries, tasks, doodles, thoughts, ideas, to-dos, or anything you don't want to forget.

Free Your Spirit

Big or small. Today or in your lifetime.

1. _____

2. _____

3. _____

4. _____

5. _____

Describe the small actions you could take to inch closer to the things you want.

NOW CLOSE YOUR EYES

Visualize taking these small actions.

Feel deeply what it feels like to do these things and move closer to what you desire.

This trains your body, mind, and spirit to help you take these actions.

Settle Your Body

Ground yourself in the present moment to get comfortable in your own skin.

☐ Take a deep breath

☐ Put your hands on your heart and say "I'm okay, I'm safe, I'm loved"

☐ What's one thing you can

See _____ Hear _____

Touch _____ Smell _____

☐ In one word, I feel... _____

☐ I deserve a High 5 today because _____

☐ The next time you pass a mirror, prove it. Give yourself a High 5!

Clear Your Mind

To cultivate a confident mind, clear it of everything that's filling it right now: worries, tasks, doodles, thoughts, ideas, to-dos, or anything you don't want to forget.

Free Your Spirit

Big or small. Today or in your lifetime.

1. _____

2. _____

3. _____

4. _____

5. _____

Describe the small actions you could take to inch closer to the things you want.

NOW CLOSE YOUR EYES

Visualize taking these small actions.

Feel deeply what it feels like to do these things and move closer to what you desire.

This trains your body, mind, and spirit to help you take these actions.

Settle Your Body

Ground yourself in the present moment to get comfortable in your own skin.

☐   Take a deep breath

☐   Put your hands on your heart and say "I'm okay, I'm safe, I'm loved"

☐   What's one thing you can

See _____   Hear _____

Touch _____   Smell _____

☐   In one word, I feel... _____

☐   I deserve a High 5 today because _____

☐   The next time you pass a mirror, prove it. Give yourself a High 5! 👏

Clear Your Mind

To cultivate a confident mind, clear it of everything that's filling it right now: worries, tasks, doodles, thoughts, ideas, to-dos, or anything you don't want to forget.

Free Your Spirit

Big or small. Today or in your lifetime.

1. _____

2. _____

3. _____

4. _____

5. _____

Describe the small actions you could take to inch closer to the things you want.

NOW CLOSE YOUR EYES

Visualize taking these small actions.

Feel deeply what it feels like to do these things and move closer to what you desire.

This trains your body, mind, and spirit to help you take these actions.

You're doing an amazing job.
Do you feel the powerful self-love and
self-confidence building?

WE'RE ALL IN THIS TOGETHER.

Give yourself a High 5 in
the mirror, take a photo,
share it online, and tag me:

@melrobbins

@melrobbins

CHEER YOURSELF FORWARD

Daily applause should be the soundtrack of your life because YOU are worth cheering for. You are a triumph. Your life is glorious. I want you to truly see and celebrate yourself. It is the single greatest gift you'll ever give yourself. It is the invitation your dreams have been waiting for.

Settle Your Body

Ground yourself in the present moment to get comfortable in your own skin.

- [ ] Take a deep breath
- [ ] Put your hands on your heart and say "I'm okay, I'm safe, I'm loved"
- [ ] What's one thing you can

  See _____   Hear _____

  Touch _____   Smell _____

- [ ] In one word, I feel... _____

- [ ] I deserve a High 5 today because _____

- [ ] The next time you pass a mirror, prove it. Give yourself a High 5! 🖐

Clear Your Mind

To cultivate a confident mind, clear it of everything that's filling it right now: worries, tasks, doodles, thoughts, ideas, to-dos, or anything you don't want to forget.

- ▪
- ▪
- ▪
- ▪
- ▪
- ▪
- ▪
- ▪
- ▪

Free Your Spirit

Big or small. Today or in your lifetime.

1. _____

2. _____

3. _____

4. _____

5. _____

Describe the small actions you could take to inch closer to the things you want.

NOW CLOSE YOUR EYES

Visualize taking these small actions.
Feel deeply what it feels like to do these things and move closer to what you desire.
This trains your body, mind, and spirit to help you take these actions.

Settle Your Body

Ground yourself in the present moment to get comfortable in your own skin.

☐ Take a deep breath

☐ Put your hands on your heart and say "I'm okay, I'm safe, I'm loved"

☐ What's one thing you can

See _____   Hear _____

Touch _____   Smell _____

☐ In one word, I feel... _____

☐ I deserve a High 5 today because _____

☐ The next time you pass a mirror, prove it. Give yourself a High 5!

Clear Your Mind

To cultivate a confident mind, clear it of everything that's filling it right now: worries, tasks, doodles, thoughts, ideas, to-dos, or anything you don't want to forget.

Free Your Spirit

Big or small. Today or in your lifetime.

1. _____

2. _____

3. _____

4. _____

5. _____

Describe the small actions you could take to inch closer to the things you want.

-
-
-
-
-
-
-
-

NOW CLOSE YOUR EYES

Visualize taking these small actions.
Feel deeply what it feels like to do these things and move closer to what you desire.
This trains your body, mind, and spirit to help you take these actions.

Settle Your Body

Ground yourself in the present moment to get comfortable in your own skin.

☐ Take a deep breath

☐ Put your hands on your heart and say "I'm okay, I'm safe, I'm loved"

☐ What's one thing you can

See _____   Hear _____

Touch _____   Smell _____

☐ In one word, I feel... _____

☐ I deserve a High 5 today because _____

☐ The next time you pass a mirror, prove it. Give yourself a High 5!

Clear Your Mind

To cultivate a confident mind, clear it of everything that's filling it right now: worries, tasks, doodles, thoughts, ideas, to-dos, or anything you don't want to forget.

Free Your Spirit

Big or small. Today or in your lifetime.

1. _____

2. _____

3. _____

4. _____

5. _____

Describe the small actions you could take to inch closer to the things you want.

NOW CLOSE YOUR EYES

Visualize taking these small actions.
Feel deeply what it feels like to do these things and move closer to what you desire.
This trains your body, mind, and spirit to help you take these actions.

Settle Your Body

Ground yourself in the present moment to get comfortable in your own skin.

- Take a deep breath
- Put your hands on your heart and say "I'm okay, I'm safe, I'm loved"
- What's one thing you can

  See _____   Hear _____

  Touch _____   Smell _____

- In one word, I feel... _____
- I deserve a High 5 today because _____
- The next time you pass a mirror, prove it. Give yourself a High 5!

Clear Your Mind

To cultivate a confident mind, clear it of everything that's filling it right now: worries, tasks, doodles, thoughts, ideas, to-dos, or anything you don't want to forget.

Free Your Spirit

Big or small. Today or in your lifetime.

1. _____

2. _____

3. _____

4. _____

5. _____

Describe the small actions you could take to inch closer to the things you want.

NOW CLOSE YOUR EYES

Visualize taking these small actions.
Feel deeply what it feels like to do these things and move closer to what you desire.
This trains your body, mind, and spirit to help you take these actions.

Settle Your Body

Ground yourself in the present moment to get comfortable in your own skin.

☐ Take a deep breath

☐ Put your hands on your heart and say "I'm okay, I'm safe, I'm loved"

☐ What's one thing you can

See _____   Hear _____

Touch _____   Smell _____

☐ In one word, I feel... _____

☐ I deserve a High 5 today because _____

☐ The next time you pass a mirror, prove it. Give yourself a High 5!

Clear Your Mind

To cultivate a confident mind, clear it of everything that's filling it right now: worries, tasks, doodles, thoughts, ideas, to-dos, or anything you don't want to forget.

Free Your Spirit

Big or small. Today or in your lifetime.

1. _____

2. _____

3. _____

4. _____

5. _____

Describe the small actions you could take to inch closer to the things you want.

-
-
-
-
-
-
-
-

NOW CLOSE YOUR EYES

Visualize taking these small actions.
Feel deeply what it feels like to do these things and move closer to what you desire.
This trains your body, mind, and spirit to help you take these actions.

Settle Your Body

Ground yourself in the present moment to get comfortable in your own skin.

- Take a deep breath
- Put your hands on your heart and say "I'm okay, I'm safe, I'm loved"
- What's one thing you can

See _____   Hear _____

Touch _____   Smell _____

- In one word, I feel... _____

- I deserve a High 5 today because _____

- The next time you pass a mirror, prove it. Give yourself a High 5!

Clear Your Mind

To cultivate a confident mind, clear it of everything that's filling it right now: worries, tasks, doodles, thoughts, ideas, to-dos, or anything you don't want to forget.

Free Your Spirit

WRITE 5 THINGS YOU WANT:

Big or small. Today or in your lifetime.

1. _____

2. _____

3. _____

4. _____

5. _____

Describe the small actions you could take to inch closer to the things you want.

NOW CLOSE YOUR EYES

Visualize taking these small actions.
Feel deeply what it feels like to do these things and move closer to what you desire.
This trains your body, mind, and spirit to help you take these actions.

Settle Your Body

Ground yourself in the present moment to get comfortable in your own skin.

- Take a deep breath
- Put your hands on your heart and say "I'm okay, I'm safe, I'm loved"
- What's one thing you can

See _____   Hear _____

Touch _____   Smell _____

- In one word, I feel... _____
- I deserve a High 5 today because _____
- The next time you pass a mirror, prove it. Give yourself a High 5!

Clear Your Mind

To cultivate a confident mind, clear it of everything that's filling it right now: worries, tasks, doodles, thoughts, ideas, to-dos, or anything you don't want to forget.

Free Your Spirit

Big or small. Today or in your lifetime.

1. _____

2. _____

3. _____

4. _____

5. _____

Describe the small actions you could take to inch closer to the things you want.

NOW CLOSE YOUR EYES

Visualize taking these small actions.

Feel deeply what it feels like to do these things and move closer to what you desire.

This trains your body, mind, and spirit to help you take these actions.

Another week done!
You're gaining momentum.
Awesome job.

Keep cheering
yourself forward.
Tag me when you do.

@melrobbins

TELL YOURSELF WHAT YOU NEED TO HEAR

You can work hard while being soft with your soul. You can take chances, screw up, and learn the lesson without burying yourself in shame. You can have huge ambitions and still treat yourself with gentle kindness. The best thing you can do is be on your own side.

Settle Your Body

Ground yourself in the present moment to get comfortable in your own skin.

- Take a deep breath
- Put your hands on your heart and say "I'm okay, I'm safe, I'm loved"
- What's one thing you can

See _____ Hear _____

Touch _____ Smell _____

- In one word, I feel... _____
- I deserve a High 5 today because _____
- The next time you pass a mirror, prove it. Give yourself a High 5!

Clear Your Mind

To cultivate a confident mind, clear it of everything that's filling it right now: worries, tasks, doodles, thoughts, ideas, to-dos, or anything you don't want to forget.

Free Your Spirit

Big or small. Today or in your lifetime.

1. _____

2. _____

3. _____

4. _____

5. _____

Describe the small actions you could take to inch closer to the things you want.

NOW CLOSE YOUR EYES

Visualize taking these small actions.
Feel deeply what it feels like to do these things and move closer to what you desire.
This trains your body, mind, and spirit to help you take these actions.

Settle Your Body

Ground yourself in the present moment to get comfortable in your own skin.

- Take a deep breath
- Put your hands on your heart and say "I'm okay, I'm safe, I'm loved"
- What's one thing you can

See _____   Hear _____

Touch _____   Smell _____

- In one word, I feel... _____
- I deserve a High 5 today because _____
- The next time you pass a mirror, prove it. Give yourself a High 5! 👏

Clear Your Mind

To cultivate a confident mind, clear it of everything that's filling it right now: worries, tasks, doodles, thoughts, ideas, to-dos, or anything you don't want to forget.

Free Your Spirit

Big or small. Today or in your lifetime.

1. _____

2. _____

3. _____

4. _____

5. _____

Describe the small actions you could take to inch closer to the things you want.

NOW CLOSE YOUR EYES

Visualize taking these small actions.

Feel deeply what it feels like to do these things and move closer to what you desire.

This trains your body, mind, and spirit to help you take these actions.

Settle Your Body

Ground yourself in the present moment to get comfortable in your own skin.

☐ Take a deep breath

☐ Put your hands on your heart and say "I'm okay, I'm safe, I'm loved"

☐ What's one thing you can

See _____   Hear _____

Touch _____   Smell _____

☐ In one word, I feel... _____

☐ I deserve a High 5 today because _____

☐ The next time you pass a mirror, prove it. Give yourself a High 5! 👏

Clear Your Mind

To cultivate a confident mind, clear it of everything that's filling it right now: worries, tasks, doodles, thoughts, ideas, to-dos, or anything you don't want to forget.

Free Your Spirit

Big or small. Today or in your lifetime.

1. _____

2. _____

3. _____

4. _____

5. _____

Describe the small actions you could take to inch closer to the things you want.

NOW CLOSE YOUR EYES

Visualize taking these small actions.
Feel deeply what it feels like to do these things and move closer to what you desire.
This trains your body, mind, and spirit to help you take these actions.

Settle Your Body

Ground yourself in the present moment to get comfortable in your own skin.

- Take a deep breath
- Put your hands on your heart and say "I'm okay, I'm safe, I'm loved"
- What's one thing you can

See _____   Hear _____

Touch _____   Smell _____

- In one word, I feel... _____
- I deserve a High 5 today because _____
- The next time you pass a mirror, prove it. Give yourself a High 5! 👏

Clear Your Mind

To cultivate a confident mind, clear it of everything that's filling it right now: worries, tasks, doodles, thoughts, ideas, to-dos, or anything you don't want to forget.

Free Your Spirit

Big or small. Today or in your lifetime.

1. _____

2. _____

3. _____

4. _____

5. _____

Describe the small actions you could take to inch closer to the things you want.

-
-
-
-
-
-
-

NOW CLOSE YOUR EYES

Visualize taking these small actions.

Feel deeply what it feels like to do these things and move closer to what you desire.

This trains your body, mind, and spirit to help you take these actions.

Settle Your Body

Ground yourself in the present moment to get comfortable in your own skin.

- Take a deep breath
- Put your hands on your heart and say "I'm okay, I'm safe, I'm loved"
- What's one thing you can

See _____   Hear _____

Touch _____   Smell _____

- In one word, I feel... _____
- I deserve a High 5 today because _____
- The next time you pass a mirror, prove it. Give yourself a High 5! 👐

Clear Your Mind

To cultivate a confident mind, clear it of everything that's filling it right now: worries, tasks, doodles, thoughts, ideas, to-dos, or anything you don't want to forget.

Free Your Spirit

Big or small. Today or in your lifetime.

1. _____

2. _____

3. _____

4. _____

5. _____

Describe the small actions you could take to inch closer to the things you want.

NOW CLOSE YOUR EYES

Visualize taking these small actions.
Feel deeply what it feels like to do these things and move closer to what you desire.
This trains your body, mind, and spirit to help you take these actions.

Settle Your Body

Ground yourself in the present moment to get comfortable in your own skin.

- Take a deep breath
- Put your hands on your heart and say "I'm okay, I'm safe, I'm loved"
- What's one thing you can

See _____   Hear _____

Touch _____   Smell _____

- In one word, I feel... _____

- I deserve a High 5 today because _____

- The next time you pass a mirror, prove it. Give yourself a High 5! 👏

Clear Your Mind

To cultivate a confident mind, clear it of everything that's filling it right now: worries, tasks, doodles, thoughts, ideas, to-dos, or anything you don't want to forget.

Free Your Spirit

Big or small. Today or in your lifetime.

1. _____

2. _____

3. _____

4. _____

5. _____

Describe the small actions you could take to inch closer to the things you want.

NOW CLOSE YOUR EYES

Visualize taking these small actions.
Feel deeply what it feels like to do these things and move closer to what you desire.
This trains your body, mind, and spirit to help you take these actions.

Settle Your Body

Ground yourself in the present moment to get comfortable in your own skin.

Take a deep breath

Put your hands on your heart and say "I'm okay, I'm safe, I'm loved"

What's one thing you can

See _____   Hear _____

Touch _____   Smell _____

In one word, I feel... _____

I deserve a High 5 today because _____

The next time you pass a mirror, prove it. Give yourself a High 5!

Clear Your Mind

To cultivate a confident mind, clear it of everything that's filling it right now: worries, tasks, doodles, thoughts, ideas, to-dos, or anything you don't want to forget.

Free Your Spirit

Big or small. Today or in your lifetime.

1. _____

2. _____

3. _____

4. _____

5. _____

Describe the small actions you could take to inch closer to the things you want.

-
-
-
-
-
-
-
-

NOW CLOSE YOUR EYES

Visualize taking these small actions.
Feel deeply what it feels like to do these things and move closer to what you desire.
This trains your body, mind, and spirit to help you take these actions.

Good for you for sticking with the High 5 Habit.
You're incredible!

Right now, give yourself a big cheer for the progress you've made. Tag me online so I can cheer along.

@melrobbins

KEEP YOUR PROMISES TO YOURSELF

When you keep the promises you make to yourself, you learn how to have your own back. This simple discipline is about doing what you said you were going to do, no matter where you are, how you feel, or who you're with. Every day, YOU decide who you want to be. You have an amazing future ahead, but it won't happen by chance. It will be created by the choices you make.

Settle Your Body

Ground yourself in the present moment to get comfortable in your own skin.

Take a deep breath

Put your hands on your heart and say "I'm okay, I'm safe, I'm loved"

What's one thing you can

See _____   Hear _____

Touch _____   Smell _____

In one word, I feel... _____

I deserve a High 5 today because _____

The next time you pass a mirror, prove it. Give yourself a High 5!

Clear Your Mind

To cultivate a confident mind, clear it of everything that's filling it right now: worries, tasks, doodles, thoughts, ideas, to-dos, or anything you don't want to forget.

Free Your Spirit

Big or small. Today or in your lifetime.

1. _____

2. _____

3. _____

4. _____

5. _____

Describe the small actions you could take to inch closer to the things you want.

-
-
-
-
-
-
-
-

NOW CLOSE YOUR EYES

Visualize taking these small actions.
Feel deeply what it feels like to do these things and move closer to what you desire.
This trains your body, mind, and spirit to help you take these actions.

Settle Your Body

Ground yourself in the present moment to get comfortable in your own skin.

Take a deep breath

Put your hands on your heart and say "I'm okay, I'm safe, I'm loved"

What's one thing you can

See _____   Hear _____

Touch _____   Smell _____

In one word, I feel... _____

I deserve a High 5 today because _____

The next time you pass a mirror, prove it. Give yourself a High 5!

Clear Your Mind

To cultivate a confident mind, clear it of everything that's filling it right now: worries, tasks, doodles, thoughts, ideas, to-dos, or anything you don't want to forget.

Free Your Spirit

Big or small. Today or in your lifetime.

1. _____

2. _____

3. _____

4. _____

5. _____

Describe the small actions you could take to inch closer to the things you want.

NOW CLOSE YOUR EYES

Visualize taking these small actions.
Feel deeply what it feels like to do these things and move closer to what you desire.
This trains your body, mind, and spirit to help you take these actions.

Settle Your Body

Ground yourself in the present moment to get comfortable in your own skin.

- Take a deep breath
- Put your hands on your heart and say "I'm okay, I'm safe, I'm loved"
- What's one thing you can

See _____   Hear _____

Touch _____   Smell _____

- In one word, I feel... _____

- I deserve a High 5 today because _____

- The next time you pass a mirror, prove it. Give yourself a High 5!

Clear Your Mind

To cultivate a confident mind, clear it of everything that's filling it right now: worries, tasks, doodles, thoughts, ideas, to-dos, or anything you don't want to forget.

Free Your Spirit

Big or small. Today or in your lifetime.

1. _____

2. _____

3. _____

4. _____

5. _____

Describe the small actions you could take to inch closer to the things you want.

NOW CLOSE YOUR EYES

Visualize taking these small actions.

Feel deeply what it feels like to do these things and move closer to what you desire.

This trains your body, mind, and spirit to help you take these actions.

Settle Your Body

Ground yourself in the present moment to get comfortable in your own skin.

☐ Take a deep breath

☐ Put your hands on your heart and say "I'm okay, I'm safe, I'm loved"

☐ What's one thing you can

See _____ Hear _____

Touch _____ Smell _____

☐ In one word, I feel... _____

☐ I deserve a High 5 today because _____

☐ The next time you pass a mirror, prove it. Give yourself a High 5! 👏

Clear Your Mind

To cultivate a confident mind, clear it of everything that's filling it right now: worries, tasks, doodles, thoughts, ideas, to-dos, or anything you don't want to forget.

▪

▪

▪

▪

▪

▪

▪

▪

Free Your Spirit

Big or small. Today or in your lifetime.

1. _____

2. _____

3. _____

4. _____

5. _____

Describe the small actions you could take to inch closer to the things you want.

NOW CLOSE YOUR EYES

Visualize taking these small actions.
Feel deeply what it feels like to do these things and move closer to what you desire.
This trains your body, mind, and spirit to help you take these actions.

Settle Your Body

Ground yourself in the present moment to get comfortable in your own skin.

- Take a deep breath
- Put your hands on your heart and say "I'm okay, I'm safe, I'm loved"
- What's one thing you can

See _____   Hear _____

Touch _____   Smell _____

- In one word, I feel... _____
- I deserve a High 5 today because _____
- The next time you pass a mirror, prove it. Give yourself a High 5!

Clear Your Mind

To cultivate a confident mind, clear it of everything that's filling it right now: worries, tasks, doodles, thoughts, ideas, to-dos, or anything you don't want to forget.

Free Your Spirit

Big or small. Today or in your lifetime.

1. _____

2. _____

3. _____

4. _____

5. _____

Describe the small actions you could take to inch closer to the things you want.

NOW CLOSE YOUR EYES

Visualize taking these small actions.

Feel deeply what it feels like to do these things and move closer to what you desire.

This trains your body, mind, and spirit to help you take these actions.

Settle Your Body

Ground yourself in the present moment to get comfortable in your own skin.

- Take a deep breath
- Put your hands on your heart and say "I'm okay, I'm safe, I'm loved"
- What's one thing you can

See _____   Hear _____

Touch _____   Smell _____

- In one word, I feel... _____
- I deserve a High 5 today because _____
- The next time you pass a mirror, prove it. Give yourself a High 5!

Clear Your Mind

To cultivate a confident mind, clear it of everything that's filling it right now: worries, tasks, doodles, thoughts, ideas, to-dos, or anything you don't want to forget.

Free Your Spirit

Big or small. Today or in your lifetime.

1. _____

2. _____

3. _____

4. _____

5. _____

Describe the small actions you could take to inch closer to the things you want.

NOW CLOSE YOUR EYES

Visualize taking these small actions.

Feel deeply what it feels like to do these things and move closer to what you desire.

This trains your body, mind, and spirit to help you take these actions.

Settle Your Body

Ground yourself in the present moment to get comfortable in your own skin.

Take a deep breath

Put your hands on your heart and say "I'm okay, I'm safe, I'm loved"

What's one thing you can

See _____   Hear _____

Touch _____   Smell _____

In one word, I feel... _____

I deserve a High 5 today because _____

The next time you pass a mirror, prove it. Give yourself a High 5!

Clear Your Mind

To cultivate a confident mind, clear it of everything that's filling it right now: worries, tasks, doodles, thoughts, ideas, to-dos, or anything you don't want to forget.

Free Your Spirit

WRITE 5 THINGS YOU WANT:

Big or small. Today or in your lifetime.

1. _____

2. _____

3. _____

4. _____

5. _____

Describe the small actions you could take to inch closer to the things you want.

NOW CLOSE YOUR EYES

Visualize taking these small actions.

Feel deeply what it feels like to do these things and move closer to what you desire.

This trains your body, mind, and spirit to help you take these actions.

You're halfway through the journal!
And I'm right here with you,
every step of the way.

Tag me online so I can give
you a virtual High 5.

#High5Challenge

@melrobbins

THERE'S SOMETHING INCREDIBLE MEANT FOR YOU

Your DNA sequence, your fingerprints, your voice, the patterns of your iris—every one of these things is entirely unique to you. Each one of your distinctive gifts and talents is a phenomenon. This is the reason you long to be seen, heard, and celebrated. To show the world who you are and what you're made of.

Settle Your Body

Ground yourself in the present moment to get comfortable in your own skin.

☐ Take a deep breath

☐ Put your hands on your heart and say "I'm okay, I'm safe, I'm loved"

☐ What's one thing you can

See _____   Hear _____

Touch _____   Smell _____

☐ In one word, I feel... _____

☐ I deserve a High 5 today because _____

☐ The next time you pass a mirror, prove it. Give yourself a High 5! 👐

Clear Your Mind

To cultivate a confident mind, clear it of everything that's filling it right now: worries, tasks, doodles, thoughts, ideas, to-dos, or anything you don't want to forget.

Free Your Spirit

Big or small. Today or in your lifetime.

1. _____

2. _____

3. _____

4. _____

5. _____

Describe the small actions you could take to inch closer to the things you want.

-
-
-
-
-
-
-

NOW CLOSE YOUR EYES

Visualize taking these small actions.
Feel deeply what it feels like to do these things and move closer to what you desire.
This trains your body, mind, and spirit to help you take these actions.

Settle Your Body

Ground yourself in the present moment to get comfortable in your own skin.

- Take a deep breath
- Put your hands on your heart and say "I'm okay, I'm safe, I'm loved"
- What's one thing you can

See _____   Hear _____

Touch _____   Smell _____

- In one word, I feel... _____

- I deserve a High 5 today because _____

- The next time you pass a mirror, prove it. Give yourself a High 5! 👏

Clear Your Mind

To cultivate a confident mind, clear it of everything that's filling it right now: worries, tasks, doodles, thoughts, ideas, to-dos, or anything you don't want to forget.

Free Your Spirit

Big or small. Today or in your lifetime.

1. _____

2. _____

3. _____

4. _____

5. _____

Describe the small actions you could take to inch closer to the things you want.

NOW CLOSE YOUR EYES

Visualize taking these small actions.
Feel deeply what it feels like to do these things and move closer to what you desire.
This trains your body, mind, and spirit to help you take these actions.

Settle Your Body

Ground yourself in the present moment to get comfortable in your own skin.

- Take a deep breath
- Put your hands on your heart and say "I'm okay, I'm safe, I'm loved"
- What's one thing you can

See _____   Hear _____

Touch _____   Smell _____

- In one word, I feel... _____
- I deserve a High 5 today because _____
- The next time you pass a mirror, prove it. Give yourself a High 5! 👏

Clear Your Mind

To cultivate a confident mind, clear it of everything that's filling it right now: worries, tasks, doodles, thoughts, ideas, to-dos, or anything you don't want to forget.

Free Your Spirit

Big or small. Today or in your lifetime.

1. _____

2. _____

3. _____

4. _____

5. _____

Describe the small actions you could take to inch closer to the things you want.

NOW CLOSE YOUR EYES

Visualize taking these small actions.
Feel deeply what it feels like to do these things and move closer to what you desire.
This trains your body, mind, and spirit to help you take these actions.

Settle Your Body

Ground yourself in the present moment to get comfortable in your own skin.

☐ Take a deep breath

☐ Put your hands on your heart and say "I'm okay, I'm safe, I'm loved"

☐ What's one thing you can

See _____   Hear _____

Touch _____   Smell _____

☐ In one word, I feel... _____

☐ I deserve a High 5 today because _____

☐ The next time you pass a mirror, prove it. Give yourself a High 5!

Clear Your Mind

To cultivate a confident mind, clear it of everything that's filling it right now: worries, tasks, doodles, thoughts, ideas, to-dos, or anything you don't want to forget.

Free Your Spirit

Big or small. Today or in your lifetime.

1. _____

2. _____

3. _____

4. _____

5. _____

Describe the small actions you could take to inch closer to the things you want.

NOW CLOSE YOUR EYES

Visualize taking these small actions.
Feel deeply what it feels like to do these things and move closer to what you desire.
This trains your body, mind, and spirit to help you take these actions.

Settle Your Body

Ground yourself in the present moment to get comfortable in your own skin.

- Take a deep breath
- Put your hands on your heart and say "I'm okay, I'm safe, I'm loved"
- What's one thing you can

  See _____   Hear _____

  Touch _____   Smell _____

- In one word, I feel... _____

- I deserve a High 5 today because _____

- The next time you pass a mirror, prove it. Give yourself a High 5! 🖐

Clear Your Mind

To cultivate a confident mind, clear it of everything that's filling it right now: worries, tasks, doodles, thoughts, ideas, to-dos, or anything you don't want to forget.

Free Your Spirit

Big or small. Today or in your lifetime.

1. _____

2. _____

3. _____

4. _____

5. _____

Describe the small actions you could take to inch closer to the things you want.

NOW CLOSE YOUR EYES

Visualize taking these small actions.
Feel deeply what it feels like to do these things and move closer to what you desire.
This trains your body, mind, and spirit to help you take these actions.

Settle Your Body

Ground yourself in the present moment to get comfortable in your own skin.

- Take a deep breath
- Put your hands on your heart and say "I'm okay, I'm safe, I'm loved"
- What's one thing you can

See _____   Hear _____

Touch _____   Smell _____

- In one word, I feel... _____
- I deserve a High 5 today because _____
- The next time you pass a mirror, prove it. Give yourself a High 5! 👏

Clear Your Mind

To cultivate a confident mind, clear it of everything that's filling it right now: worries, tasks, doodles, thoughts, ideas, to-dos, or anything you don't want to forget.

Free Your Spirit

Big or small. Today or in your lifetime.

1. _____

2. _____

3. _____

4. _____

5. _____

Describe the small actions you could take to inch closer to the things you want.

-
-
-
-
-
-
-
-

NOW CLOSE YOUR EYES

Visualize taking these small actions.
Feel deeply what it feels like to do these things and move closer to what you desire.
This trains your body, mind, and spirit to help you take these actions.

Settle Your Body

Ground yourself in the present moment to get comfortable in your own skin.

- [ ] Take a deep breath
- [ ] Put your hands on your heart and say "I'm okay, I'm safe, I'm loved"
- [ ] What's one thing you can

  See _____   Hear _____

  Touch _____   Smell _____

- [ ] In one word, I feel... _____

- [ ] I deserve a High 5 today because _____

- [ ] The next time you pass a mirror, prove it. Give yourself a High 5! 🙌

Clear Your Mind

To cultivate a confident mind, clear it of everything that's filling it right now: worries, tasks, doodles, thoughts, ideas, to-dos, or anything you don't want to forget.

Free Your Spirit

Big or small. Today or in your lifetime.

1. _____

2. _____

3. _____

4. _____

5. _____

Describe the small actions you could take to inch closer to the things you want.

-
-
-
-
-
-
-
-

NOW CLOSE YOUR EYES

Visualize taking these small actions.
Feel deeply what it feels like to do these things and move closer to what you desire.
This trains your body, mind, and spirit to help you take these actions.

You are doing SUCH an amazing job.
These small, daily steps
make a huge impact.
High 5!

Snap a pic of yourself and
your happiest High 5.
Tag me online so I can send
one right back to you.

@melrobbins

UNLOCK YOUR PURPOSE

Your purpose on earth is to show up as the REAL you. To blaze a trail and squeeze as much joy out of your life as you can. When you learn how to create an authentic life, you inspire others to do the same, and you will make a difference in someone's life. That's your power.

Settle Your Body

Ground yourself in the present moment to get comfortable in your own skin.

- Take a deep breath
- Put your hands on your heart and say "I'm okay, I'm safe, I'm loved"
- What's one thing you can

See _____   Hear _____

Touch _____   Smell _____

- In one word, I feel... _____
- I deserve a High 5 today because _____
- The next time you pass a mirror, prove it. Give yourself a High 5!

Clear Your Mind

To cultivate a confident mind, clear it of everything that's filling it right now: worries, tasks, doodles, thoughts, ideas, to-dos, or anything you don't want to forget.

Free Your Spirit

Big or small. Today or in your lifetime.

1. _____

2. _____

3. _____

4. _____

5. _____

Describe the small actions you could take to inch closer to the things you want.

Visualize taking these small actions.
Feel deeply what it feels like to do these things and move closer to what you desire.
This trains your body, mind, and spirit to help you take these actions.

Settle Your Body

Ground yourself in the present moment to get comfortable in your own skin.

- [ ] Take a deep breath
- [ ] Put your hands on your heart and say "I'm okay, I'm safe, I'm loved"
- [ ] What's one thing you can

  See _____   Hear _____

  Touch _____   Smell _____

- [ ] In one word, I feel... _____

- [ ] I deserve a High 5 today because _____

- [ ] The next time you pass a mirror, prove it. Give yourself a High 5! 👏

Clear Your Mind

To cultivate a confident mind, clear it of everything that's filling it right now: worries, tasks, doodles, thoughts, ideas, to-dos, or anything you don't want to forget.

Free Your Spirit

WRITE 5 THINGS YOU WANT:

Big or small. Today or in your lifetime.

1. _____

2. _____

3. _____

4. _____

5. _____

Describe the small actions you could take to inch closer to the things you want.

-
-
-
-
-
-
-
-

NOW CLOSE YOUR EYES

Visualize taking these small actions.
Feel deeply what it feels like to do these things and move closer to what you desire.
This trains your body, mind, and spirit to help you take these actions.

Settle Your Body

Ground yourself in the present moment to get comfortable in your own skin.

- Take a deep breath
- Put your hands on your heart and say "I'm okay, I'm safe, I'm loved"
- What's one thing you can

See _____   Hear _____

Touch _____   Smell _____

- In one word, I feel... _____
- I deserve a High 5 today because _____
- The next time you pass a mirror, prove it. Give yourself a High 5!

Clear Your Mind

To cultivate a confident mind, clear it of everything that's filling it right now: worries, tasks, doodles, thoughts, ideas, to-dos, or anything you don't want to forget.

Free Your Spirit

Big or small. Today or in your lifetime.

1. _____

2. _____

3. _____

4. _____

5. _____

Describe the small actions you could take to inch closer to the things you want.

NOW CLOSE YOUR EYES

Visualize taking these small actions.
Feel deeply what it feels like to do these things and move closer to what you desire.
This trains your body, mind, and spirit to help you take these actions.

Settle Your Body

Ground yourself in the present moment to get comfortable in your own skin.

- Take a deep breath
- Put your hands on your heart and say "I'm okay, I'm safe, I'm loved"
- What's one thing you can

See _____ Hear _____

Touch _____ Smell _____

- In one word, I feel... _____
- I deserve a High 5 today because _____
- The next time you pass a mirror, prove it. Give yourself a High 5! 👏

Clear Your Mind

To cultivate a confident mind, clear it of everything that's filling it right now: worries, tasks, doodles, thoughts, ideas, to-dos, or anything you don't want to forget.

Free Your Spirit

Big or small. Today or in your lifetime.

1. _____

2. _____

3. _____

4. _____

5. _____

Describe the small actions you could take to inch closer to the things you want.

NOW CLOSE YOUR EYES

Visualize taking these small actions.
Feel deeply what it feels like to do these things and move closer to what you desire.
This trains your body, mind, and spirit to help you take these actions.

Settle Your Body

Ground yourself in the present moment to get comfortable in your own skin.

- Take a deep breath
- Put your hands on your heart and say "I'm okay, I'm safe, I'm loved"
- What's one thing you can

See _____   Hear _____

Touch _____   Smell _____

- In one word, I feel... _____
- I deserve a High 5 today because _____
- The next time you pass a mirror, prove it. Give yourself a High 5! 👏

Clear Your Mind

To cultivate a confident mind, clear it of everything that's filling it right now: worries, tasks, doodles, thoughts, ideas, to-dos, or anything you don't want to forget.

Free Your Spirit

WRITE 5 THINGS YOU WANT:

Big or small. Today or in your lifetime.

1. _____

2. _____

3. _____

4. _____

5. _____

Describe the small actions you could take to inch closer to the things you want.

NOW CLOSE YOUR EYES

Visualize taking these small actions.

Feel deeply what it feels like to do these things and move closer to what you desire. This trains your body, mind, and spirit to help you take these actions.

Settle Your Body

Ground yourself in the present moment to get comfortable in your own skin.

☐ Take a deep breath

☐ Put your hands on your heart and say "I'm okay, I'm safe, I'm loved"

☐ What's one thing you can

See _____ Hear _____

Touch _____ Smell _____

☐ In one word, I feel... _____

☐ I deserve a High 5 today because _____

☐ The next time you pass a mirror, prove it. Give yourself a High 5! 👏

Clear Your Mind

To cultivate a confident mind, clear it of everything that's filling it right now: worries, tasks, doodles, thoughts, ideas, to-dos, or anything you don't want to forget.

▪

▪

▪

▪

▪

▪

▪

▪

▪

Free Your Spirit

WRITE 5 THINGS YOU WANT:

Big or small. Today or in your lifetime.

1. _____

2. _____

3. _____

4. _____

5. _____

Describe the small actions you could take to inch closer to the things you want.

-
-
-
-
-
-
-
-

NOW CLOSE YOUR EYES

Visualize taking these small actions.
Feel deeply what it feels like to do these things and move closer to what you desire.
This trains your body, mind, and spirit to help you take these actions.

Settle Your Body

Ground yourself in the present moment to get comfortable in your own skin.

☐ Take a deep breath

☐ Put your hands on your heart and say "I'm okay, I'm safe, I'm loved"

☐ What's one thing you can

See _____   Hear _____

Touch _____   Smell _____

☐ In one word, I feel... _____

☐ I deserve a High 5 today because _____

☐ The next time you pass a mirror, prove it. Give yourself a High 5!

Clear Your Mind

To cultivate a confident mind, clear it of everything that's filling it right now: worries, tasks, doodles, thoughts, ideas, to-dos, or anything you don't want to forget.

Free Your Spirit

Big or small. Today or in your lifetime.

1. _____

2. _____

3. _____

4. _____

5. _____

Describe the small actions you could take to inch closer to the things you want.

NOW CLOSE YOUR EYES

Visualize taking these small actions.

Feel deeply what it feels like to do these things and move closer to what you desire.

This trains your body, mind, and spirit to help you take these actions.

I'm so proud of you for making it this far.

LET ME CELEBRATE YOU.

Take a photo with your journal, post it, and tag me online

@melrobbins

so I can give you a huge shout out.

@melrobbins

YOU ARE RESILIENT

You can't change what happened to you in the past, but you can choose what happens next. It's beautiful to know that your indomitable human spirit will just NOT let you quit. You are built to go the distance in this life.

Settle Your Body

Ground yourself in the present moment to get comfortable in your own skin.

- [ ] Take a deep breath
- [ ] Put your hands on your heart and say "I'm okay, I'm safe, I'm loved"
- [ ] What's one thing you can

See _____   Hear _____

Touch _____   Smell _____

- [ ] In one word, I feel... _____

- [ ] I deserve a High 5 today because _____

- [ ] The next time you pass a mirror, prove it. Give yourself a High 5! 👐

Clear Your Mind

To cultivate a confident mind, clear it of everything that's filling it right now: worries, tasks, doodles, thoughts, ideas, to-dos, or anything you don't want to forget.

Free Your Spirit

Big or small. Today or in your lifetime.

1. _____

2. _____

3. _____

4. _____

5. _____

Describe the small actions you could take to inch closer to the things you want.

-
-
-
-
-
-
-

NOW CLOSE YOUR EYES

Visualize taking these small actions.
Feel deeply what it feels like to do these things and move closer to what you desire.
This trains your body, mind, and spirit to help you take these actions.

Settle Your Body

Ground yourself in the present moment to get comfortable in your own skin.

- Take a deep breath
- Put your hands on your heart and say "I'm okay, I'm safe, I'm loved"
- What's one thing you can

See _____   Hear _____

Touch _____   Smell _____

- In one word, I feel... _____

- I deserve a High 5 today because _____

- The next time you pass a mirror, prove it. Give yourself a High 5! 👏

Clear Your Mind

To cultivate a confident mind, clear it of everything that's filling it right now: worries, tasks, doodles, thoughts, ideas, to-dos, or anything you don't want to forget.

Free Your Spirit

Big or small. Today or in your lifetime.

1. _____

2. _____

3. _____

4. _____

5. _____

Describe the small actions you could take to inch closer to the things you want.

NOW CLOSE YOUR EYES

Visualize taking these small actions.
Feel deeply what it feels like to do these things and move closer to what you desire.
This trains your body, mind, and spirit to help you take these actions.

Settle Your Body

Ground yourself in the present moment to get comfortable in your own skin.

- Take a deep breath
- Put your hands on your heart and say "I'm okay, I'm safe, I'm loved"
- What's one thing you can

  See _____   Hear _____

  Touch _____   Smell _____

- In one word, I feel... _____
- I deserve a High 5 today because _____
- The next time you pass a mirror, prove it. Give yourself a High 5! 👏

Clear Your Mind

To cultivate a confident mind, clear it of everything that's filling it right now: worries, tasks, doodles, thoughts, ideas, to-dos, or anything you don't want to forget.

Free Your Spirit

Big or small. Today or in your lifetime.

1. _____

2. _____

3. _____

4. _____

5. _____

Describe the small actions you could take to inch closer to the things you want.

NOW CLOSE YOUR EYES

Visualize taking these small actions.

Feel deeply what it feels like to do these things and move closer to what you desire.

This trains your body, mind, and spirit to help you take these actions.

Settle Your Body

Ground yourself in the present moment to get comfortable in your own skin.

- Take a deep breath
- Put your hands on your heart and say "I'm okay, I'm safe, I'm loved"
- What's one thing you can

See _____ Hear _____

Touch _____ Smell _____

- In one word, I feel... _____
- I deserve a High 5 today because _____
- The next time you pass a mirror, prove it. Give yourself a High 5! 👏

Clear Your Mind

To cultivate a confident mind, clear it of everything that's filling it right now: worries, tasks, doodles, thoughts, ideas, to-dos, or anything you don't want to forget.

Free Your Spirit

WRITE 5 THINGS YOU WANT:

Big or small. Today or in your lifetime.

1. _____

2. _____

3. _____

4. _____

5. _____

Describe the small actions you could take to inch closer to the things you want.

-
-
-
-
-
-
-
-

NOW CLOSE YOUR EYES

Visualize taking these small actions.
Feel deeply what it feels like to do these things and move closer to what you desire.
This trains your body, mind, and spirit to help you take these actions.

Settle Your Body

Ground yourself in the present moment to get comfortable in your own skin.

- Take a deep breath
- Put your hands on your heart and say "I'm okay, I'm safe, I'm loved"
- What's one thing you can

  See _____   Hear _____

  Touch _____   Smell _____

- In one word, I feel... _____

- I deserve a High 5 today because _____

- The next time you pass a mirror, prove it. Give yourself a High 5! 👐

Clear Your Mind

To cultivate a confident mind, clear it of everything that's filling it right now: worries, tasks, doodles, thoughts, ideas, to-dos, or anything you don't want to forget.

Free Your Spirit

Big or small. Today or in your lifetime.

1. _____

2. _____

3. _____

4. _____

5. _____

Describe the small actions you could take to inch closer to the things you want.

NOW CLOSE YOUR EYES

Visualize taking these small actions.

Feel deeply what it feels like to do these things and move closer to what you desire.

This trains your body, mind, and spirit to help you take these actions.

Settle Your Body

Ground yourself in the present moment to get comfortable in your own skin.

☐ Take a deep breath

☐ Put your hands on your heart and say "I'm okay, I'm safe, I'm loved"

☐ What's one thing you can

See _____   Hear _____

Touch _____   Smell _____

☐ In one word, I feel... _____

☐ I deserve a High 5 today because _____

☐ The next time you pass a mirror, prove it. Give yourself a High 5! 👏

Clear Your Mind

To cultivate a confident mind, clear it of everything that's filling it right now: worries, tasks, doodles, thoughts, ideas, to-dos, or anything you don't want to forget.

Free Your Spirit

Big or small. Today or in your lifetime.

1. _____

2. _____

3. _____

4. _____

5. _____

Describe the small actions you could take to inch closer to the things you want.

NOW CLOSE YOUR EYES

Visualize taking these small actions.
Feel deeply what it feels like to do these things and move closer to what you desire.
This trains your body, mind, and spirit to help you take these actions.

Settle Your Body

Ground yourself in the present moment to get comfortable in your own skin.

☐ Take a deep breath

☐ Put your hands on your heart and say "I'm okay, I'm safe, I'm loved"

☐ What's one thing you can

See _____   Hear _____

Touch _____   Smell _____

☐ In one word, I feel... _____

☐ I deserve a High 5 today because _____

☐ The next time you pass a mirror, prove it. Give yourself a High 5! 👏

Clear Your Mind

To cultivate a confident mind, clear it of everything that's filling it right now: worries, tasks, doodles, thoughts, ideas, to-dos, or anything you don't want to forget.

Free Your Spirit

Big or small. Today or in your lifetime.

1. _____

2. _____

3. _____

4. _____

5. _____

Describe the small actions you could take to inch closer to the things you want.

-

-

-

-

-

-

-

-

NOW CLOSE YOUR EYES

Visualize taking these small actions.

Feel deeply what it feels like to do these things and move closer to what you desire.

This trains your body, mind, and spirit to help you take these actions.

You are fantastic. Another week in the books!
What are you doing to celebrate?

Let me know online:

#High5Challenge

I want to hear your stories!

TAKE
ACTION

You cannot think your way to a new life. You must act your way there. It's going to require simple discipline that comes from practicing new habits. If you want your life to be different, you've got to start acting differently. You are never too old, never too young, and it's never too late to find the power to change absolutely everything.

Settle Your Body

Ground yourself in the present moment to get comfortable in your own skin.

- [ ] Take a deep breath
- [ ] Put your hands on your heart and say "I'm okay, I'm safe, I'm loved"
- [ ] What's one thing you can

  See _____   Hear _____

  Touch _____   Smell _____

- [ ] In one word, I feel... _____
- [ ] I deserve a High 5 today because _____
- [ ] The next time you pass a mirror, prove it. Give yourself a High 5! 🙌

Clear Your Mind

To cultivate a confident mind, clear it of everything that's filling it right now: worries, tasks, doodles, thoughts, ideas, to-dos, or anything you don't want to forget.

- ▪
- ▪
- ▪
- ▪
- ▪
- ▪
- ▪
- ▪
- ▪

Free Your Spirit

Big or small. Today or in your lifetime.

1. _____

2. _____

3. _____

4. _____

5. _____

Describe the small actions you could take to inch closer to the things you want.

-
-
-
-
-
-
-
-

NOW CLOSE YOUR EYES

Visualize taking these small actions.
Feel deeply what it feels like to do these things and move closer to what you desire.
This trains your body, mind, and spirit to help you take these actions.

Settle Your Body

Ground yourself in the present moment to get comfortable in your own skin.

☐ Take a deep breath

☐ Put your hands on your heart and say "I'm okay, I'm safe, I'm loved"

☐ What's one thing you can

See _____ Hear _____

Touch _____ Smell _____

☐ In one word, I feel... _____

☐ I deserve a High 5 today because _____

☐ The next time you pass a mirror, prove it. Give yourself a High 5!

Clear Your Mind

To cultivate a confident mind, clear it of everything that's filling it right now: worries, tasks, doodles, thoughts, ideas, to-dos, or anything you don't want to forget.

Free Your Spirit

WRITE 5 THINGS YOU WANT:

Big or small. Today or in your lifetime.

1. _____

2. _____

3. _____

4. _____

5. _____

Describe the small actions you could take to inch closer to the things you want.

NOW CLOSE YOUR EYES

Visualize taking these small actions.

Feel deeply what it feels like to do these things and move closer to what you desire.

This trains your body, mind, and spirit to help you take these actions.

Settle Your Body

Ground yourself in the present moment to get comfortable in your own skin.

☐ Take a deep breath

☐ Put your hands on your heart and say "I'm okay, I'm safe, I'm loved"

☐ What's one thing you can

See _____ Hear _____

Touch _____ Smell _____

☐ In one word, I feel... _____

☐ I deserve a High 5 today because _____

☐ The next time you pass a mirror, prove it. Give yourself a High 5!

Clear Your Mind

To cultivate a confident mind, clear it of everything that's filling it right now: worries, tasks, doodles, thoughts, ideas, to-dos, or anything you don't want to forget.

Free Your Spirit

Big or small. Today or in your lifetime.

1. _____

2. _____

3. _____

4. _____

5. _____

Describe the small actions you could take to inch closer to the things you want.

NOW CLOSE YOUR EYES

Visualize taking these small actions.
Feel deeply what it feels like to do these things and move closer to what you desire.
This trains your body, mind, and spirit to help you take these actions.

Settle Your Body

Ground yourself in the present moment to get comfortable in your own skin.

☐ Take a deep breath

☐ Put your hands on your heart and say "I'm okay, I'm safe, I'm loved"

☐ What's one thing you can

See _____ Hear _____

Touch _____ Smell _____

☐ In one word, I feel... _____

☐ I deserve a High 5 today because _____

☐ The next time you pass a mirror, prove it. Give yourself a High 5!

Clear Your Mind

To cultivate a confident mind, clear it of everything that's filling it right now: worries, tasks, doodles, thoughts, ideas, to-dos, or anything you don't want to forget.

Free Your Spirit

Big or small. Today or in your lifetime.

1. _____

2. _____

3. _____

4. _____

5. _____

Describe the small actions you could take to inch closer to the things you want.

-
-
-
-
-
-
-
-

NOW CLOSE YOUR EYES

Visualize taking these small actions.
Feel deeply what it feels like to do these things and move closer to what you desire.
This trains your body, mind, and spirit to help you take these actions.

Settle Your Body

Ground yourself in the present moment to get comfortable in your own skin.

- Take a deep breath
- Put your hands on your heart and say "I'm okay, I'm safe, I'm loved"
- What's one thing you can

See _____   Hear _____

Touch _____   Smell _____

- In one word, I feel... _____
- I deserve a High 5 today because _____
- The next time you pass a mirror, prove it. Give yourself a High 5! 👏

Clear Your Mind

To cultivate a confident mind, clear it of everything that's filling it right now: worries, tasks, doodles, thoughts, ideas, to-dos, or anything you don't want to forget.

Free Your Spirit

Big or small. Today or in your lifetime.

1. _____

2. _____

3. _____

4. _____

5. _____

Describe the small actions you could take to inch closer to the things you want.

NOW CLOSE YOUR EYES

Visualize taking these small actions.
Feel deeply what it feels like to do these things and move closer to what you desire.
This trains your body, mind, and spirit to help you take these actions.

Settle Your Body

Ground yourself in the present moment to get comfortable in your own skin.

- Take a deep breath
- Put your hands on your heart and say "I'm okay, I'm safe, I'm loved"
- What's one thing you can

See _____   Hear _____

Touch _____   Smell _____

- In one word, I feel... _____
- I deserve a High 5 today because _____
- The next time you pass a mirror, prove it. Give yourself a High 5!

Clear Your Mind

To cultivate a confident mind, clear it of everything that's filling it right now: worries, tasks, doodles, thoughts, ideas, to-dos, or anything you don't want to forget.

Free Your Spirit

Big or small. Today or in your lifetime.

1. _____

2. _____

3. _____

4. _____

5. _____

Describe the small actions you could take to inch closer to the things you want.

-
-
-
-
-
-
-
-

NOW CLOSE YOUR EYES

Visualize taking these small actions.

Feel deeply what it feels like to do these things and move closer to what you desire.

This trains your body, mind, and spirit to help you take these actions.

Settle Your Body

Ground yourself in the present moment to get comfortable in your own skin.

- Take a deep breath
- Put your hands on your heart and say "I'm okay, I'm safe, I'm loved"
- What's one thing you can

See _____   Hear _____

Touch _____   Smell _____

- In one word, I feel... _____
- I deserve a High 5 today because _____
- The next time you pass a mirror, prove it. Give yourself a High 5!

Clear Your Mind

To cultivate a confident mind, clear it of everything that's filling it right now: worries, tasks, doodles, thoughts, ideas, to-dos, or anything you don't want to forget.

Free Your Spirit

Big or small. Today or in your lifetime.

1. _____

2. _____

3. _____

4. _____

5. _____

Describe the small actions you could take to inch closer to the things you want.

-
-
-
-
-
-
-
-

NOW CLOSE YOUR EYES

Visualize taking these small actions.
Feel deeply what it feels like to do these things and move closer to what you desire.
This trains your body, mind, and spirit to help you take these actions.

Congratulations. You've made giving yourself a High 5 a habit.

Want to join people around the world who are all doing the same? We're right here at

High5Challenge.com

(YES. I'M PART OF IT TOO!)

@melrobbins

KNOW THAT YOU ARE WORTHY

We spend so much of our lives attaching our worth to things outside ourselves that we start to believe we are only worthy of love or celebration when we get that win, that raise, or that praise. The truth is, you are worthy just as you are. You were born worthy. Every day when you wake up, practice cheering for YOU. Don't wait another minute to lift yourself up.

Settle Your Body

Ground yourself in the present moment to get comfortable in your own skin.

- Take a deep breath
- Put your hands on your heart and say "I'm okay, I'm safe, I'm loved"
- What's one thing you can

  See _____   Hear _____

  Touch _____   Smell _____

- In one word, I feel... _____
- I deserve a High 5 today because _____
- The next time you pass a mirror, prove it. Give yourself a High 5!

Clear Your Mind

To cultivate a confident mind, clear it of everything that's filling it right now: worries, tasks, doodles, thoughts, ideas, to-dos, or anything you don't want to forget.

Free Your Spirit

Big or small. Today or in your lifetime.

1. _____

2. _____

3. _____

4. _____

5. _____

Describe the small actions you could take to inch closer to the things you want.

NOW CLOSE YOUR EYES

Visualize taking these small actions.
Feel deeply what it feels like to do these things and move closer to what you desire.
This trains your body, mind, and spirit to help you take these actions.

Settle Your Body

Ground yourself in the present moment to get comfortable in your own skin.

- [ ] Take a deep breath
- [ ] Put your hands on your heart and say "I'm okay, I'm safe, I'm loved"
- [ ] What's one thing you can

See _____ Hear _____

Touch _____ Smell _____

- [ ] In one word, I feel... _____
- [ ] I deserve a High 5 today because _____
- [ ] The next time you pass a mirror, prove it. Give yourself a High 5! 👐

Clear Your Mind

To cultivate a confident mind, clear it of everything that's filling it right now: worries, tasks, doodles, thoughts, ideas, to-dos, or anything you don't want to forget.

Free Your Spirit

Big or small. Today or in your lifetime.

1. _____

2. _____

3. _____

4. _____

5. _____

Describe the small actions you could take to inch closer to the things you want.

NOW CLOSE YOUR EYES

Visualize taking these small actions.

Feel deeply what it feels like to do these things and move closer to what you desire.

This trains your body, mind, and spirit to help you take these actions.

Settle Your Body

Ground yourself in the present moment to get comfortable in your own skin.

Take a deep breath

Put your hands on your heart and say "I'm okay, I'm safe, I'm loved"

What's one thing you can

See _____   Hear _____

Touch _____   Smell _____

In one word, I feel... _____

I deserve a High 5 today because _____

The next time you pass a mirror, prove it. Give yourself a High 5!

Clear Your Mind

To cultivate a confident mind, clear it of everything that's filling it right now: worries, tasks, doodles, thoughts, ideas, to-dos, or anything you don't want to forget.

Free Your Spirit

Big or small. Today or in your lifetime.

1. _____

2. _____

3. _____

4. _____

5. _____

Describe the small actions you could take to inch closer to the things you want.

-
-
-
-
-
-
-
-

NOW CLOSE YOUR EYES

Visualize taking these small actions.
Feel deeply what it feels like to do these things and move closer to what you desire.
This trains your body, mind, and spirit to help you take these actions.

Settle Your Body

Ground yourself in the present moment to get comfortable in your own skin.

☐ Take a deep breath

☐ Put your hands on your heart and say "I'm okay, I'm safe, I'm loved"

☐ What's one thing you can

See _____   Hear _____

Touch _____   Smell _____

☐ In one word, I feel... _____

☐ I deserve a High 5 today because _____

☐ The next time you pass a mirror, prove it. Give yourself a High 5!

Clear Your Mind

To cultivate a confident mind, clear it of everything that's filling it right now: worries, tasks, doodles, thoughts, ideas, to-dos, or anything you don't want to forget.

Free Your Spirit

Big or small. Today or in your lifetime.

1. _____

2. _____

3. _____

4. _____

5. _____

Describe the small actions you could take to inch closer to the things you want.

-
-
-
-
-
-
-

NOW CLOSE YOUR EYES

Visualize taking these small actions.

Feel deeply what it feels like to do these things and move closer to what you desire.

This trains your body, mind, and spirit to help you take these actions.

Settle Your Body

Ground yourself in the present moment to get comfortable in your own skin.

☐ Take a deep breath

☐ Put your hands on your heart and say "I'm okay, I'm safe, I'm loved"

☐ What's one thing you can

See _____   Hear _____

Touch _____   Smell _____

☐ In one word, I feel... _____

☐ I deserve a High 5 today because _____

☐ The next time you pass a mirror, prove it. Give yourself a High 5! 👏

Clear Your Mind

To cultivate a confident mind, clear it of everything that's filling it right now: worries, tasks, doodles, thoughts, ideas, to-dos, or anything you don't want to forget.

-
-
-
-
-
-
-
-
-

Free Your Spirit

WRITE 5 THINGS YOU WANT:

Big or small. Today or in your lifetime.

1. _____

2. _____

3. _____

4. _____

5. _____

Describe the small actions you could take to inch closer to the things you want.

-

-

-

-

-

-

-

NOW CLOSE YOUR EYES

Visualize taking these small actions.
Feel deeply what it feels like to do these things and move closer to what you desire.
This trains your body, mind, and spirit to help you take these actions.

Settle Your Body

Ground yourself in the present moment to get comfortable in your own skin.

- Take a deep breath
- Put your hands on your heart and say "I'm okay, I'm safe, I'm loved"
- What's one thing you can

See _____   Hear _____

Touch _____   Smell _____

- In one word, I feel... _____

- I deserve a High 5 today because _____

- The next time you pass a mirror, prove it. Give yourself a High 5!

Clear Your Mind

To cultivate a confident mind, clear it of everything that's filling it right now: worries, tasks, doodles, thoughts, ideas, to-dos, or anything you don't want to forget.

Free Your Spirit

WRITE 5 THINGS YOU WANT:

Big or small. Today or in your lifetime.

1. _____

2. _____

3. _____

4. _____

5. _____

Describe the small actions you could take to inch closer to the things you want.

NOW CLOSE YOUR EYES

Visualize taking these small actions.
Feel deeply what it feels like to do these things and move closer to what you desire.
This trains your body, mind, and spirit to help you take these actions.

Settle Your Body

Ground yourself in the present moment to get comfortable in your own skin.

- Take a deep breath
- Put your hands on your heart and say "I'm okay, I'm safe, I'm loved"
- What's one thing you can

See _____   Hear _____

Touch _____   Smell _____

- In one word, I feel... _____
- I deserve a High 5 today because _____
- The next time you pass a mirror, prove it. Give yourself a High 5!

Clear Your Mind

To cultivate a confident mind, clear it of everything that's filling it right now: worries, tasks, doodles, thoughts, ideas, to-dos, or anything you don't want to forget.

Free Your Spirit

Big or small. Today or in your lifetime.

1. _____

2. _____

3. _____

4. _____

5. _____

Describe the small actions you could take to inch closer to the things you want.

-
-
-
-
-
-
-
-

NOW CLOSE YOUR EYES

Visualize taking these small actions.

Feel deeply what it feels like to do these things and move closer to what you desire.

This trains your body, mind, and spirit to help you take these actions.

I'm proud of you for <u>sticking</u> with this.

Now take a photo of yourself and tag me

@melrobbins

because I want to cheer right along with you.

@melrobbins

GO AHEAD AND WANT THINGS

You get to want things. You deserve to be happy. In fact, happiness, just like your dreams, is your birthright. You were born to want things, and wanting them fuels the energy of your spirit. It gives your spirit direction so it knows which way to soar. So say what you want and conjure the confidence to believe you will have it.

Settle Your Body

Ground yourself in the present moment to get comfortable in your own skin.

- Take a deep breath
- Put your hands on your heart and say "I'm okay, I'm safe, I'm loved"
- What's one thing you can

See _____   Hear _____

Touch _____   Smell _____

- In one word, I feel... _____
- I deserve a High 5 today because _____
- The next time you pass a mirror, prove it. Give yourself a High 5!

Clear Your Mind

To cultivate a confident mind, clear it of everything that's filling it right now: worries, tasks, doodles, thoughts, ideas, to-dos, or anything you don't want to forget.

Free Your Spirit

Big or small. Today or in your lifetime.

1. _____

2. _____

3. _____

4. _____

5. _____

Describe the small actions you could take to inch closer to the things you want.

NOW CLOSE YOUR EYES

Visualize taking these small actions.
Feel deeply what it feels like to do these things and move closer to what you desire.
This trains your body, mind, and spirit to help you take these actions.

Settle Your Body

Ground yourself in the present moment to get comfortable in your own skin.

- Take a deep breath
- Put your hands on your heart and say "I'm okay, I'm safe, I'm loved"
- What's one thing you can

See _____   Hear _____

Touch _____   Smell _____

- In one word, I feel... _____

- I deserve a High 5 today because _____

- The next time you pass a mirror, prove it. Give yourself a High 5! 👏

Clear Your Mind

To cultivate a confident mind, clear it of everything that's filling it right now: worries, tasks, doodles, thoughts, ideas, to-dos, or anything you don't want to forget.

Free Your Spirit

Big or small. Today or in your lifetime.

1. _____

2. _____

3. _____

4. _____

5. _____

Describe the small actions you could take to inch closer to the things you want.

-
-
-
-
-
-
-
-

NOW CLOSE YOUR EYES

Visualize taking these small actions.
Feel deeply what it feels like to do these things and move closer to what you desire.
This trains your body, mind, and spirit to help you take these actions.

Settle Your Body

Ground yourself in the present moment to get comfortable in your own skin.

- [ ] Take a deep breath
- [ ] Put your hands on your heart and say "I'm okay, I'm safe, I'm loved"
- [ ] What's one thing you can

  See _____   Hear _____

  Touch _____   Smell _____

- [ ] In one word, I feel... _____
- [ ] I deserve a High 5 today because _____
- [ ] The next time you pass a mirror, prove it. Give yourself a High 5! 👏

Clear Your Mind

To cultivate a confident mind, clear it of everything that's filling it right now: worries, tasks, doodles, thoughts, ideas, to-dos, or anything you don't want to forget.

Free Your Spirit

Big or small. Today or in your lifetime.

1. _____

2. _____

3. _____

4. _____

5. _____

Describe the small actions you could take to inch closer to the things you want.

NOW CLOSE YOUR EYES

Visualize taking these small actions.
Feel deeply what it feels like to do these things and move closer to what you desire.
This trains your body, mind, and spirit to help you take these actions.

Settle Your Body

Ground yourself in the present moment to get comfortable in your own skin.

- Take a deep breath
- Put your hands on your heart and say "I'm okay, I'm safe, I'm loved"
- What's one thing you can

See _____   Hear _____

Touch _____   Smell _____

- In one word, I feel... _____
- I deserve a High 5 today because _____
- The next time you pass a mirror, prove it. Give yourself a High 5!

Clear Your Mind

To cultivate a confident mind, clear it of everything that's filling it right now: worries, tasks, doodles, thoughts, ideas, to-dos, or anything you don't want to forget.

Free Your Spirit

Big or small. Today or in your lifetime.

1. _____
2. _____
3. _____
4. _____
5. _____

Describe the small actions you could take to inch closer to the things you want.

-
-
-
-
-
-
-
-

NOW CLOSE YOUR EYES

Visualize taking these small actions.
Feel deeply what it feels like to do these things and move closer to what you desire.
This trains your body, mind, and spirit to help you take these actions.

Settle Your Body

Ground yourself in the present moment to get comfortable in your own skin.

- Take a deep breath
- Put your hands on your heart and say "I'm okay, I'm safe, I'm loved"
- What's one thing you can

See _____   Hear _____

Touch _____   Smell _____

- In one word, I feel... _____
- I deserve a High 5 today because _____
- The next time you pass a mirror, prove it. Give yourself a High 5!

Clear Your Mind

To cultivate a confident mind, clear it of everything that's filling it right now: worries, tasks, doodles, thoughts, ideas, to-dos, or anything you don't want to forget.

Free Your Spirit

WRITE 5 THINGS YOU WANT:

Big or small. Today or in your lifetime.

1. _____

2. _____

3. _____

4. _____

5. _____

Describe the small actions you could take to inch closer to the things you want.

NOW CLOSE YOUR EYES

Visualize taking these small actions.

Feel deeply what it feels like to do these things and move closer to what you desire.

This trains your body, mind, and spirit to help you take these actions.

Settle Your Body

Ground yourself in the present moment to get comfortable in your own skin.

☐ Take a deep breath

☐ Put your hands on your heart and say "I'm okay, I'm safe, I'm loved"

☐ What's one thing you can

See _____   Hear _____

Touch _____   Smell _____

☐ In one word, I feel... _____

☐ I deserve a High 5 today because _____

☐ The next time you pass a mirror, prove it. Give yourself a High 5! ✋

Clear Your Mind

To cultivate a confident mind, clear it of everything that's filling it right now: worries, tasks, doodles, thoughts, ideas, to-dos, or anything you don't want to forget.

Free Your Spirit

Big or small. Today or in your lifetime.

1. _____

2. _____

3. _____

4. _____

5. _____

Describe the small actions you could take to inch closer to the things you want.

NOW CLOSE YOUR EYES

Visualize taking these small actions.
Feel deeply what it feels like to do these things and move closer to what you desire.
This trains your body, mind, and spirit to help you take these actions.

Settle Your Body

Ground yourself in the present moment to get comfortable in your own skin.

☐ Take a deep breath

☐ Put your hands on your heart and say "I'm okay, I'm safe, I'm loved"

☐ What's one thing you can

See _____   Hear _____

Touch _____   Smell _____

☐ In one word, I feel... _____

☐ I deserve a High 5 today because _____

☐ The next time you pass a mirror, prove it. Give yourself a High 5!

Clear Your Mind

To cultivate a confident mind, clear it of everything that's filling it right now: worries, tasks, doodles, thoughts, ideas, to-dos, or anything you don't want to forget.

Free Your Spirit

Big or small. Today or in your lifetime.

1. _____

2. _____

3. _____

4. _____

5. _____

Describe the small actions you could take to inch closer to the things you want.

NOW CLOSE YOUR EYES

Visualize taking these small actions.

Feel deeply what it feels like to do these things and move closer to what you desire.

This trains your body, mind, and spirit to help you take these actions.

You did it!

This is the last week of
The High 5 Daily Journal.

IT'S TIME TO CELEBRATE.

Take a picture of yourself
giving me a High 5,
post it online and tag me

@melrobbins

#High5Challenge

so I can cheer for YOU!

@melrobbins

BUILD YOUR CONFIDENCE: BODY, MIND, AND SPIRIT

Trust is a major component of confidence. Trust in your dreams, your intuition, your abilities, and in the divine nature of things. Trust that everything in your life is preparing you for something that hasn't happened yet. You may not be able to see how all the dots connect, but confidence is knowing that at some point in this beautiful life of yours, it will all make perfect, even magical sense.

Settle Your Body

Ground yourself in the present moment to get comfortable in your own skin.

- [ ] Take a deep breath
- [ ] Put your hands on your heart and say "I'm okay, I'm safe, I'm loved"
- [ ] What's one thing you can

  See _____   Hear _____

  Touch _____   Smell _____

- [ ] In one word, I feel... _____
- [ ] I deserve a High 5 today because _____
- [ ] The next time you pass a mirror, prove it. Give yourself a High 5! 👐

Clear Your Mind

To cultivate a confident mind, clear it of everything that's filling it right now: worries, tasks, doodles, thoughts, ideas, to-dos, or anything you don't want to forget.

Free Your Spirit

WRITE 5 THINGS YOU WANT:

Big or small. Today or in your lifetime.

1. _____

2. _____

3. _____

4. _____

5. _____

Describe the small actions you could take to inch closer to the things you want.

NOW CLOSE YOUR EYES

Visualize taking these small actions.

Feel deeply what it feels like to do these things and move closer to what you desire.
This trains your body, mind, and spirit to help you take these actions.

Settle Your Body

Ground yourself in the present moment to get comfortable in your own skin.

☐ Take a deep breath

☐ Put your hands on your heart and say "I'm okay, I'm safe, I'm loved"

☐ What's one thing you can

See _____   Hear _____

Touch _____   Smell _____

☐ In one word, I feel... _____

☐ I deserve a High 5 today because _____

☐ The next time you pass a mirror, prove it. Give yourself a High 5! 👏

Clear Your Mind

To cultivate a confident mind, clear it of everything that's filling it right now: worries, tasks, doodles, thoughts, ideas, to-dos, or anything you don't want to forget.

Free Your Spirit

Big or small. Today or in your lifetime.

1. _____

2. _____

3. _____

4. _____

5. _____

Describe the small actions you could take to inch closer to the things you want.

NOW CLOSE YOUR EYES

Visualize taking these small actions.
Feel deeply what it feels like to do these things and move closer to what you desire.
This trains your body, mind, and spirit to help you take these actions.

Settle Your Body

Ground yourself in the present moment to get comfortable in your own skin.

- Take a deep breath
- Put your hands on your heart and say "I'm okay, I'm safe, I'm loved"
- What's one thing you can

  See _____   Hear _____

  Touch _____   Smell _____

- In one word, I feel... _____

- I deserve a High 5 today because _____

- The next time you pass a mirror, prove it. Give yourself a High 5! 👏

Clear Your Mind

To cultivate a confident mind, clear it of everything that's filling it right now: worries, tasks, doodles, thoughts, ideas, to-dos, or anything you don't want to forget.

Free Your Spirit

Big or small. Today or in your lifetime.

1. _____

2. _____

3. _____

4. _____

5. _____

Describe the small actions you could take to inch closer to the things you want.

NOW CLOSE YOUR EYES

Visualize taking these small actions.

Feel deeply what it feels like to do these things and move closer to what you desire.

This trains your body, mind, and spirit to help you take these actions.

Settle Your Body

Ground yourself in the present moment to get comfortable in your own skin.

☐ Take a deep breath

☐ Put your hands on your heart and say "I'm okay, I'm safe, I'm loved"

☐ What's one thing you can

See _____ Hear _____

Touch _____ Smell _____

☐ In one word, I feel... _____

☐ I deserve a High 5 today because _____

☐ The next time you pass a mirror, prove it. Give yourself a High 5! 🖐️

Clear Your Mind

To cultivate a confident mind, clear it of everything that's filling it right now: worries, tasks, doodles, thoughts, ideas, to-dos, or anything you don't want to forget.

Free Your Spirit

Big or small. Today or in your lifetime.

1. _____

2. _____

3. _____

4. _____

5. _____

Describe the small actions you could take to inch closer to the things you want.

NOW CLOSE YOUR EYES

Visualize taking these small actions.
Feel deeply what it feels like to do these things and move closer to what you desire.
This trains your body, mind, and spirit to help you take these actions.

Settle Your Body

Ground yourself in the present moment to get comfortable in your own skin.

- Take a deep breath
- Put your hands on your heart and say "I'm okay, I'm safe, I'm loved"
- What's one thing you can

  See _____   Hear _____

  Touch _____   Smell _____

- In one word, I feel... _____

- I deserve a High 5 today because _____

- The next time you pass a mirror, prove it. Give yourself a High 5! 👏

Clear Your Mind

To cultivate a confident mind, clear it of everything that's filling it right now: worries, tasks, doodles, thoughts, ideas, to-dos, or anything you don't want to forget.

Free Your Spirit

Big or small. Today or in your lifetime.

1. _____

2. _____

3. _____

4. _____

5. _____

Describe the small actions you could take to inch closer to the things you want.

NOW CLOSE YOUR EYES

Visualize taking these small actions.

Feel deeply what it feels like to do these things and move closer to what you desire.

This trains your body, mind, and spirit to help you take these actions.

Settle Your Body

Ground yourself in the present moment to get comfortable in your own skin.

- Take a deep breath
- Put your hands on your heart and say "I'm okay, I'm safe, I'm loved"
- What's one thing you can

See _____ Hear _____

Touch _____ Smell _____

- In one word, I feel... _____
- I deserve a High 5 today because _____
- The next time you pass a mirror, prove it. Give yourself a High 5! 🖐

Clear Your Mind

To cultivate a confident mind, clear it of everything that's filling it right now: worries tasks, doodles, thoughts, ideas, to-dos, or anything you don't want to forget.

Free Your Spirit

Big or small. Today or in your lifetime.

1. _____

2. _____

3. _____

4. _____

5. _____

Describe the small actions you could take to inch closer to the things you want.

NOW CLOSE YOUR EYES

Visualize taking these small actions.
Feel deeply what it feels like to do these things and move closer to what you desire.
This trains your body, mind, and spirit to help you take these actions.

Settle Your Body

Ground yourself in the present moment to get comfortable in your own skin.

- Take a deep breath
- Put your hands on your heart and say "I'm okay, I'm safe, I'm loved"
- What's one thing you can

See _____   Hear _____

Touch _____   Smell _____

- In one word, I feel... _____
- I deserve a High 5 today because _____
- The next time you pass a mirror, prove it. Give yourself a High 5!

Clear Your Mind

To cultivate a confident mind, clear it of everything that's filling it right now: worries, tasks, doodles, thoughts, ideas, to-dos, or anything you don't want to forget.

Free Your Spirit

Big or small. Today or in your lifetime.

1. _____

2. _____

3. _____

4. _____

5. _____

Describe the small actions you could take to inch closer to the things you want.

NOW CLOSE YOUR EYES

Visualize taking these small actions.
Feel deeply what it feels like to do these things and move closer to what you desire.
This trains your body, mind, and spirit to help you take these actions.

Mel Robbins

Mel Robbins is the leading female voice in personal development and transformation and an international bestselling author. Mel's work includes *The High 5 Habit, The 5 Second Rule*, four #1 bestselling audiobooks, the #1 podcast on Audible, as well as signature online courses that have changed the lives of more than half a million students worldwide.

Her groundbreaking work on behavior change has been translated into 36 languages and is used by veterans' organizations, healthcare professionals, and the world's top organizations to inspire people to be more confident, effective, and fulfilled.

As one of the most widely booked public speakers in the world, Mel's coaching reaches more than 60 million people every month and videos featuring her work have more than a billion views online, including her TEDx talk, which is one of the most popular of all time.

There's nothing Mel loves more than making a real difference in people's lives, encouraging them to believe in themselves and take the actions that will propel them toward their destiny.

Mel lives in southern Vermont with her husband of 25 years and their three kids, but she is and will always be a midwesterner at heart.

WWW.MELROBBINS.COM

@melrobbins

@melrobbins

facebook.com/melrobbins

youtube.com/melrobbins

For more resources and information about the release of new editions of *The High 5 Daily Journal*, go to High5Journal.com.

Keep yourself inspired and motivated.
Join the free High 5 Challenge with people around the world at High5Challenge.com